Mathematical Learning and Understanding in Education

Mathematics holds an essential, ubiquitous presence in the education sector, as do ongoing explorations of its effective teaching and learning. Written by leading experts on mathematics and mathematics education, this book situates issues of student thinking and learning about mathematics within the broader context of educational psychology research and theory and brings them to a wider audience. With chapters on knowing and understanding mathematics, mathematical habits, early mathematical thinking, and learning mathematics, this concise volume is designed for any educational psychology, mathematics education, or general education course that includes student learning in the curriculum. It will be indispensable for student researchers and both pre- and in-service teachers alike.

Kristie Newton is Associate Professor in the Department of Teaching and Learning at Temple University, USA.

Sarah Sword is Senior Research Scientist at Education Development Center, Inc.

Ed Psych Insights
Series Editor: Patricia A. Alexander

Assessment of Student Achievement
Gavin T. L. Brown

Self-Efficacy and Future Goals in Education
Barbara Greene

Self-Regulation in Education
Jeffrey A. Greene

Strategic Processing in Education
Daniel L. Dinsmore

Cognition in Education
Matthew T. McCrudden and Danielle S. McNamara

Emotions at School
Reinhard Pekrun, Krista R. Muis, Anne C. Frenzel, and Thomas Goetz

Teacher Expectations in Education
Christine M. Rubie-Davies

Classroom Discussions in Education
Edited by P. Karen Murphy

Science Learning and Inquiry with Technology
Diane Jass Ketelhut and Michael Shane Tutwiler

Mathematical Learning and Understanding in Education
Kristie Newton and Sarah Sword

KRISTIE NEWTON AND
SARAH SWORD

Mathematical Learning and Understanding in Education

NEW YORK AND LONDON

First published 2018
by Routledge
711 Third Avenue, New York, NY 10017

and by Routledge
2 Park Square, Milton Park, Abingdon, Oxon, OX14 4RN

Routledge is an imprint of the Taylor & Francis Group, an informa business

© 2018 Taylor & Francis

The right of Kristie Newton and Sarah Sword to be identified as authors of this work has been asserted by them in accordance with sections 77 and 78 of the Copyright, Designs and Patents Act 1988.

All rights reserved. No part of this book may be reprinted or reproduced or utilised in any form or by any electronic, mechanical, or other means, now known or hereafter invented, including photocopying and recording, or in any information storage or retrieval system, without permission in writing from the publishers.

Trademark notice: Product or corporate names may be trademarks or registered trademarks, and are used only for identification and explanation without intent to infringe.

Library of Congress Cataloging-in-Publication Data
Names: Newton, Kristie Jones, 1973– author. | Sword, Sarah, author.
Title: Mathematical learning and understanding in education /
 Kristie Newton and Sarah Sword.
Description: New York, NY : Routledge, 2018. | Series: Ed psych insights |
 Includes bibliographical references and index.
Identifiers: LCCN 2017061304 (print) | LCCN 2018004385 (ebook) |
 ISBN 9781315537443 (eBook) | ISBN 9781138689138 (hardback) |
 ISBN 9781138689145 (pbk.)
Subjects: LCSH: Mathematics—Study and teaching. | Mathematics
 teachers—Training of. | Educational psychology.
Classification: LCC QA135.6 (ebook) | LCC QA135.6 .N4825 2018 (print) |
 DDC 372.7/044—dc23
LC record available at https://lccn.loc.gov/2017061304

ISBN: 978-1-138-68913-8 (hbk)
ISBN: 978-1-138-68914-5 (pbk)
ISBN: 978-1-315-53744-3 (ebk)

Typeset in Joanna MT
by Apex CoVantage, LLC

Contents

Preface		vii
Acknowledgments		xii

One: Mathematical Knowledge — 1
    Focus on Skill — 1
    Focus on Meaning — 4
    Focus on Process — 14

Two: Mathematical Habits and Practices — 24
    Introduction — 24
    Seeking and Using Structure — 33
    Using Language Clearly and Precisely — 39
    Experimenting — 43
    Conclusion — 49

Three: Children's Thinking About Mathematics — 52
    Early Awareness of Numbers — 52
    Student-Invented Procedures — 55
    Errors and Misconceptions — 62

Four:	**Learning to Solve Mathematics Problems**	**73**
	What Is a Mathematical Problem?	73
	How Do We Support Students in Learning to Solve Problems?	87
	Concluding Thoughts	98

Glossary	104
Index	108

Preface

> The issue, then, is not, What is the best way to teach? but, What is mathematics really all about? . . . Controversies about . . . teaching cannot be resolved without confronting problems about the nature of mathematics.[1]
>
> Hersh

If you ask of a variety or people to say what mathematics is, you will likely have a variety of responses. Is it a language, a tool, a science, or an art? Mathematicians generally feel that they know what mathematics is, but find it difficult to give a good direct definition. It is interesting to try, but one way of thinking about what mathematics *is* is to look at what people who use and create mathematics *do*. What are the habits and practices of mathematicians? What, then, is the nature of mathematical knowledge? And how do children think about and learn mathematics? What kinds of problems do or should they solve? In this book we provide an overview of some answers to these questions.

Our perspectives on these questions are shaped by many influences. Kristie's Ph.D. focused on educational psychology with a strong emphasis in mathematics education. Sarah's Ph.D. is in pure mathematics, with a post-doctoral fellowship in mathematics education. Our professional work crosses the three domains, and we address ideas about learning and understanding mathematics from these professional lenses. But like you, our personal stories also shape our perspectives on learning and understanding mathematics, which we share below.

Kristie: I often tell the story of my brother who went off to college two years ahead of schedule and would return during breaks only to frustrate me with what he was learning about mathematics. To be more precise, he would frustrate me by *asking me* about what he was learning. "How am I supposed to know that?" I asked. "Why are you asking me? Aren't you supposed to *tell* me?" While only one year older, he was now three years ahead in school. So what made him think I could possibly answer questions about the topics he was learning? Yet he insisted I try. His purpose was aimed not so much at the specific details of limits and sequences, for example, but at the general notion that mathematics is something that could be figured out.

His insistence paid off, however, and eventually I was hooked. I became a firm believer that mathematics was something to be understood, not just memorized. Even my senior science fair project explored mathematics learning in this vein. I surveyed people with a wide range of mathematics backgrounds using tasks that required more than rote memorization, with the purpose of understanding their thinking on these tasks. Years of tutoring during college and while teaching kept me focused on this kind of understanding. My first full-time teaching position was with an organization called Project SEED, where we were trained not to lecture but to ask questions as a way of guiding upper elementary students to think about and figure out interesting mathematical ideas they had yet to encounter in school. Students made conjectures and explained their thinking about the problems we posed. They listened to each other's ideas and respectfully argued their point. If they were unable to convince their classmates of the correct answer, we would ask more questions. What amazed me most about this experience was the speed at which students would begin to pick up on new ideas. They came to understand that mathematics was something that was supposed to make sense, and they began to look for patterns. They discovered mathematical rules and used them to build new knowledge. I took many of these ideas with me when I taught at a local high school, and I am still on this trajectory today. Indeed, this book is grounded in the notion that mathematics is not just a collection of rules, that it includes an understanding of ideas.

Based on these experiences, I have long held a deep interest in how we learn mathematics, what we are capable of learning at different ages, and what impacts that learning. Although my undergraduate work was in mathematics, I moved quickly into education prior to my graduate studies, teaching in a variety of contexts. My experiences with teaching, especially those with Project SEED, sparked my interest in educational psychology as a way to understand what I was seeing in the classroom. Through my research, teaching, and now parenting, I have continued to think about and explore what it means to understand mathematics.

Sarah: I grew up in love with numbers – I loved calculating and I loved thinking about them. My early Algebra experiences were shaped not by textbooks or by teachers, but by my best friend. In fifth grade, the first time we encountered a page of "solve for x" problems, she changed each x to a j, because her name was Jes. I was surprised by her daring, but she explained that it didn't matter what the letter was, it was just standing in for some number that we would figure out by solving the equations in front of us. Later, when we bumped into problems in which equations were representing functions, she explained that difference, too – in her (by then) middle-school language she made clear the difference between treating x as a place-holder for a number, and treating x as a variable. ("You know how you're used to x standing for *one* number?" she asked. "It could stand for *any* number, right? That variable x could actually *vary* and then this whole expression would vary, too.") It wasn't a distinction that books or our teachers made, but it was one that she made. And it was interesting, creative, and sensible.

That sense my friend instilled in me – that mathematics is interesting, creative, and sensible – has served me through a life of work in mathematics, and in my current work at Education Development Center, Inc. (EDC), a non-profit education company. Throughout this book, I draw on examples from curriculum materials, many of which are produced at EDC, and all of which are intended to foster those ideas she gave me about mathematics: it really *is* interesting, creative, and sensible. I now use the examples we share in the book in my professional work and also with my young children.

A ninth grader I (Sarah) once taught said about his own mathematics learning: "I get the how sometimes, but not the why or what. And sometimes I get the why and what, but not the how. And sometimes I get the what but not the how or why." For us, understanding mathematics involves the what, why, and how, and in this book, we treat "learning" as the process of coming to understand. We address that coming to understand from three different perspectives: mathematics education, education psychology, and mathematics as a discipline.

Toward this end, we open with a chapter on what it means to understand mathematics, what mathematics is, and how these ideas have evolved over time and impacted mathematics education. In the second chapter, we elaborate on what it is that mathematicians (experts) do, highlighting three examples of those habits. In the third chapter, we overview mathematical learning from the viewpoint of children (novices), including early and informal learning, their invented ways of solving problems, and misconceptions that underlie some common errors. Given that children in school generally learn mathematics by solving problems, the fourth chapter explores the nature and kinds of mathematical problems, as well as ways to support learning through problem solving. Throughout the book, although we do not focus per se on particular instructional approaches or curricula for learning mathematics, we see learning and instruction as highly related and therefore draw upon research and personal experiences in these areas to illuminate some of the ideas presented in the book.

That said, there are so many important issues related to learning mathematics that are largely beyond the scope of this book. These include but are not limited to beliefs about learning, motivation to learn, individual differences, stereotype threat, socioeconomic status, and curriculum. And it may seem odd that, in a book about learning and understanding, we only mention achievement a handful of times. Although ultimately we want students to achieve at mathematics, we view achievement as a measure of skill attainment whereas our primary interests lie in what children are experiencing and thinking with regard to mathematics.

NOTE

1 Hersh, R. (1979). Some proposals for reviving the philosophy of mathematics. *Advances in Mathematics*, 31, 34.

Acknowledgments

Thank you to those who provided feedback on earlier versions of the book, including Ming Tomayko, Tim Fukawa-Connelly, Jim Fey, Al Cuoco, Ryota Matsuura, and Chris Newton. All remaining mistakes are ours, of course. Thank you to the mentors who have guided us along the way, especially Pat Alexander, Christel Rotthaus, and Al Cuoco. Thanks to our families, especially to our daughters, who allowed their stories, art, and mathematical thinking to shape and inform this book.

One
Mathematical Knowledge

To some, knowing mathematics means being able to skillfully compute answers by manipulating numbers and variables. Certainly, those skills are an important part of mathematical knowledge, but many will argue it involves much more. In this chapter, we consider shifting and sometimes competing views of mathematical knowledge, including knowledge as a collection of skills, as a set of meaning concepts, and as a process of engaging in a particular way of thinking. In order to do this, we also highlight historical and theoretical influences on these three views.

FOCUS ON SKILL

"When am I ever going to use this?" We have all heard (or asked!) this question. A teacher might respond to this question by providing students with practical examples of using mathematics, such as shopping with discounts and sales tax. If you are reading this book, you probably acknowledge that mathematics is useful. Purchasing a new home, weighing the benefits of a student loan, and managing a 401K all involve some understanding of mathematics. Technical careers can involve even higher levels of mathematics. I (Kristie) asked an aerospace engineer I know for an example, and he described a mission where the main engine of a rocket had shut down 5 seconds too early. Fortunately, the engineers had asked themselves, "How much extra propellant should you budget on stage 2 of your rocket in case stage 1 has a problem?" In the end, the mission was considered a success. Of course, if a teacher responded to students' questions about using mathematics with an example about rockets, the students might in turn respond with something like, "Well, then, I don't need to learn this. I am not going to be a rocket scientist." Good point. Does that mean mathematics is not worth studying? Or does it mean students should only study what they are likely to use?

Questions about the value of learning mathematics are by no means new. In the late 1800s, mathematics was included as a traditional subject in high school, but schooling was limited for most people. Early in the twentieth century, however, mathematics education began to see a shift that reflected the rapidly growing population of students. Schools were beginning to serve the masses, with more children attending and staying in school for longer. For many, the purpose of school was vocational training for jobs where mathematics beyond an elementary level was perceived to be of little use.[1] With the purpose of school changing, mathematics was falling out of favor as a discipline, nearly disappearing from the high school curriculum because it was deemed as something the majority of people did not use to a great extent in their daily lives or even their careers. It was being replaced with courses such as home economics, art, and physical education. Indeed, the National Council of Teachers of Mathematics (NCTM) was formed in 1920 in part as a response to this trend. Given the focus on practical use of mathematics, skillful execution of algorithms was a primary emphasis.

Psychological perspectives on learning during the early part of the twentieth century also supported a focus on skill.

In particular, Edward Thorndike forwarded a behavioral view of learning whereby the student is presented with a stimulus (e.g., *fraction division problem*) and a response (e.g., *flip and multiply*), and this response is practiced and coupled with reward or punishment until the connection between the stimulus and response is well-established.[2] From this perspective, practice is an important tool for learning mathematics. Fast forward a few decades to the middle of the twentieth century, and we find further justification for the role of practice. According to information processing theory, practice can lead to automaticity, which can facilitate learning new material or solving complex problems. Within the information processing model, working memory is a component of our memory system where attending to new information happens; it is where the thinking is done. However, working memory is limited, and being able to automatically retrieve mathematical facts or algorithms from long-term memory can free up our working memory for the more complex aspects of the problem at hand. For example, converting $3\frac{7}{8}$ to $\frac{31}{8}$ can be especially challenging for a child who is unable to automatically retrieve $3 \times 8 = 24$ from long-term memory since it is merely the first step in series of steps required to do the conversion.

Whereas "skill" evokes images of number manipulation, children must also be able to interpret the mathematical symbols they are presented with. *Procedural knowledge* is an important aspect of mathematical knowledge that includes knowledge of symbols, syntax, and algorithms.[3] Knowledge of mathematical symbols and the acceptable ways of using them (i.e., syntax) comprise the "form" of mathematics, whereas algorithms are the "step-by-step instructions that prescribe how

4 Mathematical Knowledge

to complete tasks." These tasks can be either symbolic (e.g., adding two fractions) or non-symbolic (e.g., measuring an angle) in nature.

There is no doubt that mathematics involves skillful execution of procedures. Whether you are using mathematics in your professional work, learning mathematics in school, or creating new mathematics, skill is involved. When students are assessed in mathematics class or on standardized tests, it is in large part skill that is assessed. And given that new mathematics builds on prior knowledge, many skills are assessed again and again. Yet, as discussed further in Chapter 2, mathematics is clearly more than a collection of skills. In the next section, we discuss the role of meaning in mathematics learning.

FOCUS ON MEANING

> It is a mistake to suppose that meaningful arithmetic is something new, something cut out of the whole cloth, as it were, during the past twenty or twenty-five years.[4]
>
> William Brownell

> The situation in the field of understanding of ideas can only be described as serious, perhaps even desperate . . . One need only ask the average man-in-the-street whether he understood the mathematics he learnt in school: the reply will be that he carried out the teacher's instructions but that the why and wherefore was hardly ever clear.[5]
>
> Dienes

Psychologists, educators, and mathematicians have long argued for the importance of teaching "meaningful" mathematics, which emphasizes ideas and sense-making over rote memorization. Yet, the experiences of many people have highlighted computational skill, not understanding. Clearly, as this section's epigraphs note, this endeavor to imbue school mathematics with meaning is hardly trivial. William Brownell, an educational psychologist, questioned the status quo in the early part of the twentieth century, when school mathematics focused on producing answers without much concern for meaning.[6] Brownell criticized this approach on several grounds, including its lack of focus on mathematical thinking, and argued instead for a focus on the underlying ideas of the mathematics.[7]

In *The Process of Education*, psychologist Jerome Bruner argued that focusing on underlying ideas and principles make even "difficult" topics accessible to young students.[8] Consider a young child who laughs and jumps up and down with excitement when he or she sees a balloon for the first time. Although the child knows nothing formal about gravity, he or she knows objects typically go down (not up) and can therefore learn something of the idea of gravity without knowing details that an older child may be expected to memorize. Similarly, I (Kristie) once watched a kindergarten lesson on the concept of force, where the teacher tried to move a large box by blowing on it as if it were a feather. The kindergarteners laughed because they were able to intuitively understand that the box was "too heavy" to be moved with such a small force. If the teacher had instead offered a formula for calculating the amount of force needed to move the box, chances are good that it would not have gone well. However, ideas can be revisited with increasing complexity as the child develops. According to Bruner, complex knowledge must be structured or organized around fundamental ideas so it can be learned with meaning. In his words, "Grasping the structure of a subject is understanding it in a way that permits many other

6 Mathematical Knowledge

things to be related to it meaningfully. To learn structure, in short, is to learn how things are related" (p. 7).

Take for example, the rules for adding integers. Students can simply memorize which rule applies to a particular problem type. Alternatively, the rules can be developed by understanding the relationship between positive and negative numbers. Number lines can provide a helpful visual representation. In some classrooms, colored chips are used to represent negative (e.g., red) and positive (e.g., yellow) numbers and students learn that they pair up to make zero, as with -1 + 1 = 0. These kinds of pairs, also called opposites or additive inverses, can be used to make sense of integer addition. In the Project SEED classes described earlier, these pairs are usually introduced by posing a problem that cannot be solved with positive numbers, such as "What can I add to 5 to get 0?". Once students become comfortable with additive inverses and the fact that their sum is zero, instructors pose problems where they have to "look" for additive inverses and make use of them to find a missing value. Consider the following problems.

$$-4 + -5 + 4 + 5 = \square$$

$$3 + \triangle + 6 + -3 = 0$$

$$-2 + 2 + 7 = \square$$

These types of questions are used to encourage students to think about additive inverses as a helpful thing to notice. Once these kinds of problems are mastered, the instructor might pose a question like -4 + 10 = $\triangle$ and ask for conjectures. Most commonly, students offer -14 and 6. To explain the 6, a student would make use of additive inverses by decomposing the 10 into 4 + 6 so that he or she was essentially solving an

Mathematical Knowledge

equivalent problem: -4 + 4 + 6 (which, as seen above, was a familiar one). On the board, the instructor would capture this thinking:

$$-4 + 10 = ?$$

$$-4 + 4 + 6 = ?$$

$$0 + 6 = 6$$

After plenty of similar examples, students begin to answer these types of questions easily and with speed. At this point, the instructor might ask, "How did you get your answer so quickly?" Inevitably, someone would suggest that you can just subtract. In the problem above, subtract 4 from 10, and there is your sum. After confirming that this "shortcut" seemed to consistently work (because the number you subtract is always an additive inverse), instructors will challenge the students' thinking with a problem like -10 + 3 = ◇. You might guess that typical conjectures at this point are 7 and -7. And so on and so forth goes the class. Making conjectures, looking for patterns. In short, the focus is on underlying ideas (e.g., additive inverses) and how they can be used to build other ideas, such as the standard algorithms for integer addition.

Although the focus on meaning in prior decades paved the way for curriculum reform, the Soviet Union's launch of Sputnik in 1957 provided a sense of urgency to improve mathematics education in the United States. The mathematics curriculum was perceived as inadequate as a foundation for competing in the international markets.[9] Mathematicians became heavily involved in addressing this concern, writing curricula to expand and deepen the content that was introduced in the elementary and secondary schools. Further emphasizing meaning, the content introduced more abstract ideas, including logic, set theory, and number properties in ways that might make sense to younger students. Federal funds were secured to forward this process, which has been referred to as the *New Math* movement. Ultimately, these efforts were met with very limited success. With a lack of appropriate professional development, materials, or parent support of the movement, the 1970s were marked by a push to focus once again on computational skill. This next movement, referred to as *Back to Basics*, was characterized by heavy skill practice that some might argue never left the majority of schools.

A wide range of instructional strategies have since been forwarded for how to effectively teach mathematics, including the use of concrete representations, games, discourse, investigations, worked examples, and direct instruction. Many have continued to argue that the goal of any approach should be deep understanding of the mathematics, or understanding that goes beyond rote memorization. For some, deep understanding includes knowledge of why procedures and definitions make sense (e.g., Why is a negative times a negative equal to a positive number?). This distinction was important to Richard Skemp, who claimed that rote understanding isn't understanding at all but acknowledged that it is sometimes referred to in this way.[10] For example, a student might say, "I understand how to add fractions." Yet, the student may simply mean, "I know how to add fractions." If asked to explain why you need a common denominator, the student may have little to contribute. Skemp made a distinction between these meanings or uses of the word "understanding" by using different terms. He referred to *instrumental understanding* as knowing how to carry out procedures. Going back the point of practical use, this understanding might enable you to use mathematics as a tool (or instrument) in your daily life or career. If someone knows not only how to calculate an answer but also why it works that way, he or she has a *relational understanding* of the topic. In short, he or she understands the relationships between procedures and concepts. Understanding in this sense is in addition to the skill; someone with the skill for adding fractions may or may not know why it works that way.

The notion of relational understanding is similar to that of *conceptual knowledge*. A counterpart to procedural knowledge, conceptual knowledge "can be thought of as a connected web of knowledge" such that relational understanding is a prominent feature.[11] It includes specific ideas as well as broader ones that cut across contexts. With regard to adding fractions, an important idea is that equivalent fractions can be used to rename fractions-to-be-added such that their value is unchanged but the size of the parts are the same. In that case, the numerators can be added to find the total number of those parts. More broadly, it is important to understand that there are many ways to name the same amount. This "big idea" can be used to solve a variety of problems in mathematics, from fractions to algebraic and geometric problems. Both levels of understanding are considered to be conceptual in nature. Although it has long been acknowledged that conceptual and procedural knowledge do not encompass all mathematical knowledge, they have been widely used for assessing it. However, there is much inconsistency in the way that conceptual knowledge has been measured. While some researchers

10 Mathematical Knowledge

have used a broader definition that includes a relational understanding of algorithms and an ability to transfer ideas to new situations, others have used a narrower perspective (i.e., knowledge of basic concepts such as how to represent $\frac{2}{3}$ with a diagram). These differences make it challenging to compare findings on conceptual knowledge across research studies. Procedural knowledge is generally measured as computational skill.

In the last decade there has been a growing interest in what is considered by some to be "deep procedural knowledge."[12] Also described as *procedural flexibility*, this distinction builds on the idea that not all procedural knowledge is rote knowledge. It acknowledges the value that experts in mathematics place on elegance and efficiency. More specifically, procedural flexibility is the knowledge of multiple ways to solve problems along with the ability and tendency to choose the best method based on specific characteristics of the problem. An expert may use a "clear the denominator" strategy for algebra problems that involve fractions, such as $\frac{2}{3}x + \frac{1}{3} = 5$, which would override the more general approach for solving an equation. Or a flexible problem solver might, for example, notice that $\frac{2}{3} = \frac{10}{x}$ involves equivalent fractions and use this knowledge to solve the equation rather than cross multiplying to get 2x = 30 then dividing by 2. An interesting difference between flexibility and procedural knowledge as described above is in the way that it is measured. Flexibility is apparent in the way a problem is solved, not in the final solution.

Consider the following problem:

$$\frac{3}{6} + \frac{2}{4} = ?$$

The common denominator method for finding the sum is to rename each fraction using a common denominator and then add the numerators, keeping the denominator the same. This method is a standard approach for adding fractions with different denominators; it works for adding any two fractions. Another method is to notice that both fractions are equivalent to $\frac{1}{2}$ and so their sum is 1. The second method represents a special case; not all fractions can be simplified but in this case doing so makes the problem especially easy to solve. If we were only interested in whether a person could find the correct sum, both methods appear to demonstrate the same level of understanding. Yet, a solver using equivalent fractions has demonstrated knowledge and appropriate use of an important concept (e.g., fraction equivalence) to solve the problem in a more efficient manner.

At any given time, students may know of and use a variety of methods for solving problems. Consider, for example, a young child who is asked to add 3 apples to 5 apples. In order to find the total number of apples, the child may combine the sets and count all of the apples. This method is known as the *count all* method. Other times, this same child may start with 5 and count 6, 7, 8, known as the *count on* method. With greater use of the second method, the child will notice it is more efficient and begin to use it more frequently, eventually dropping the "count all" method. At the same time, he or she may begin to store 8 in memory as the sum of 3 and 5; in this case, the child may begin to solve such problems through recall of basic facts, while sometimes still using the "count on" method.

Siegler[13] described this process of competing approaches in his *Overlapping Waves Theory*. This theory can explain the movement from less mature methods that children might use

12 Mathematical Knowledge

(e.g., counting with fingers) to more sophisticated ones (e.g., recall), as well as movement from incorrect methods to correct ones. The theory has been applied to a variety of learning contexts and is consistent with the development of procedural flexibility, where students will first gain knowledge of alternative, more efficient methods prior to using them with any frequency. In the interim, they may use them sometimes but not others. Flexibility is a trait seen with experts in mathematics, who tend to use the general methods as a last resort.[14] Although younger students show a similar preference for more efficient methods, they may also be concerned with accuracy. In other words, if their method is working, there may be some resistance to switching to a new one even after acknowledging it is better in some way.

In Chapter 2, we elaborate on the use of structures as a mathematical practice; let us now highlight its role in procedural flexibility. In an interview, an algebra expert (in this case, an engineer) was asked to solve this equation:

$$\frac{1}{3}(x+5) + \frac{2}{3}(x+5) = 7$$

He first cleared the denominator by multiplying both sides of the equation by 3, then he simplified and solved the following, transformed equation by distributing and combining like terms:

$$(x+5) + 2(x+5) = 21$$

Certainly, you can argue this method is easier than distributing fractions as a first step; the engineer was flexibly applying his knowledge to solve the equation more efficiently. Yet, when asked if there was another way you could solve the problem, he was genuinely upset with himself for not initially noticing that both parentheses had the same thing in them and could therefore be combined. Moreover, $\frac{1}{3}$ of that thing plus $\frac{2}{3}$ of that same thing is equivalent to 1 of those things so that the equation simplifies to $x + 5 = 7$. In fact, he then referred to his own method as "incredibly convoluted", saying it was just instinct to clear the denominator so he didn't look beyond that feature. To him, there was great value in noticing the structure of the equation and taking advantage of it to solve the problem in the most elegant way possible. Other experts have referred to this particular use of structure as "pretty" or "clever."[15] We argue that this "clever" solution is a good example of procedural flexibility. Flexibility requires seeing underlying structures in the symbols, and research tells us that seeing these underlying structures requires conceptual knowledge. In the case of algebraic equations, it requires strong knowledge of equation features such as the equal sign, variables, negative signs, and like terms.[16]

As demonstrated, flexible knowledge involves both skill and understanding. According to mathematician Hung-Hsi Wu, "The truth is that in mathematics, skills and understanding are completely intertwined."[17] The nature of the intertwinement, however, is not without debate, and consequently, neither is the nature of instruction that should follow. There exists a long debate of concepts-first versus procedures-first for mathematics instruction that continues today, although evidence suggests that no matter which we start with, concepts and procedures build on one another.[18] I (Kristie) know my own inclination when I teach is to start with the idea, build toward the procedure, and then have students practice that procedure. But just recently, someone who in fact uses a good amount of mathematics in his profession said to me that

14 Mathematical Knowledge

he believes the understanding can come later. And I have to acknowledge it was not the first time I heard that perspective. In the following section, we highlight some of the processes involved in coming to know mathematics.

FOCUS ON PROCESS

> For generations, high school students have studied something in school that has been called mathematics, but which has very little to do with the way mathematics is created or applied outside of school.[19]
>
> Cuoco, Goldenberg, & Mark

Mathematicians have long brought attention to the stark differences between the mathematics they know and the mathematics carried out in school. Al Cuoco and his colleagues emphasize the habits of mind of mathematicians as a way to think about what kinds of experiences students should be having with mathematics. According to these mathematicians, students should be: pattern sniffers, experimenters, describers, tinkerers, inventors, visualizers, conjecturers, and even guessers. Paul Lockhart, a mathematician turned teacher, also laments in his famous essay that "it is so heartbreaking to see what is being done to mathematics in school. This rich and fascinating adventure of the imagination has been reduced to a sterile set of 'facts' to be memorized and procedures to be followed."[20]

In his essay, Lockhart contrasts two scenarios. In the first scenario, he draws a triangle inscribed in a rectangle and wonders how much of the rectangle is taken up by the triangle. After some thought he realizes that by adding one particular (dotted below) line to the image he can determine that the triangle takes up half of the rectangle because it creates two smaller rectangles, each one cut in half.

Mathematical Knowledge 15

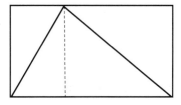

In the second scenario, he presents a triangle, along with the formula for finding its area.

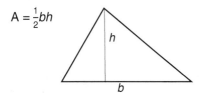

He argues that this scenario is more often the one encountered by students, and it leaves little room for actual engagement with mathematics. He suggests it *both poses the question and answers* it. How much area does a triangle take up? It takes up half of the space of a rectangle with the same base and height. In Chapter 2, experimenting is presented as an important, perhaps even critical, mathematical practice. In the triangle problem, it can lead to an understanding of the relationship between a rectangle and a triangle. Or, in Skemp's terms, it leads to a relational understanding of the area formula for a triangle. You might argue (as some certainly have) that it would be easier just to show students how you can use a line to find the area of the triangle. After all, this would still provide meaning over rote memorization and it would take less time from other tasks. But Lockhart placed high value on the process of coming to understand, in this case through experimenting. He acknowledged that algorithms are important and necessary but insisted that participation in the processes that lead to understanding is at the heart of doing mathematics.

Process has also been emphasized in several of the NCTM documents. In the latter part of the twentieth century, NCTM advocated not only for the inclusion of mathematics as an important part of the K–12 curriculum, but for the expansion of our conceptions of what it means to do mathematics. With these documents, the focus shifted to problem solving and student thinking about mathematics. In particular, the process standards set forth in their 2000 document, *Principles and Standards for School Mathematics*, described mathematical endeavors that go beyond computation to include problem solving, reasoning and proof, communication, connections, and representation.[21] In other words, mathematics is not just about computing. Students should be finding solutions and justifying their thinking. Students should be discussing their ideas orally and in writing. They should make connections to the real world, to other subject areas, and to other mathematics topics. Finally, students should be able to represent mathematical ideas in a variety of ways and be able to move easily between these representations. These process-focused standards helped to form what has been known as the Standards Movement.

The movement towards Standards brought forth curricula that were called "Standards-based," meaning that they were supposed to be aligned with the Standards laid out in the new guidelines. The National Science Foundation supported the development of a spate of curricula for all grade levels in several waves of development. These new curricula represented a variety of ideas, some of which were radically different from what came before in the United States. For example, some (but not all) of the new approaches to high school mathematics curricula were "integrated," rather than being separated into the traditional Algebra 1–Geometry–Algebra 2 course. After all, an engineer doesn't solve Algebra problems or Geometry problems; he or she uses whatever mathematics is appropriate for the task at hand. Elementary and middle school curricula often incorporated a new focus on early algebraic thinking. And keeping in mind lessons learned in the "New Math" era, most programs also developed significant professional development programs for teachers who were implementing the new programs. Many of these curricula continue to be in wide use today, and some of the "new" ideas and approaches they brought to bear have been picked up by "traditional" programs, too.

Not everyone was pleased with this movement, however. For some, attempts to counter the drill of basic skills went too far, focusing on *conceptual understanding* at the expense of procedural skill. Calculator use was emphasized. Students were encouraged to create their own ways of solving problems. Textbooks often lacked specific rules to follow, since students were encouraged to make sense of problems and find ways to solve them. Parents complained that they were ill-equipped to help with homework. Mathematicians complained that reform curricula lacked rigor. These philosophical differences and debates that ensued have been referred to as the *Math Wars*.[22] Is mathematics about understanding ideas? Skillful execution of algorithms? Particular kinds of practices?

In *Adding it Up* (2001),[23] a book aimed at (but not entirely successful at) resolving the so-called Math Wars, a diverse group of people, including mathematicians, mathematics educators, and psychologists, described mathematics as an integration of processes, skill, and understanding. According to the authors, there is some truth in each of these perspectives. They suggest that *mathematical proficiency* involves five related strands: conceptual understanding, *procedural fluency*, *strategic competence*, *adaptive reasoning*, and a *productive disposition* about mathematics. Conceptual understanding is sometimes used interchangeably with conceptual knowledge or deep understanding. It includes understanding how different mathematical ideas are related, how they are represented, and when they are useful. Procedural fluency involves knowledge of procedures as well as skill with using them both accurately and flexibly. Strategic competence means being able to represent a problem mathematically. The rocket problem at the beginning of the chapter not only involved understanding calculus but being able to make use of it to help ensure the mission was successful. In other words, when mathematical situations arise in real contexts, the formula doesn't make itself available to you; it is up to you to represent the situation mathematically. Adaptive reasoning is the logical thought – the mathematical glue, if you will – needed to justify mathematical moves. Finally, a student will not likely learn without seeing mathematics as something worthwhile, understandable, and achievable. I (Kristie) still recall one algebra student for whom, for six weeks, the primary goal was to convince him to stop crumpling up his paper and throwing it on the floor. He had struggled with mathematics for so long, that his mind was made up. He was convinced he just could not do it, so he refused to try. To say he lacked a productive disposition is an understatement. But once he decided that effort would pay off, he began to do his work and gain competence and confidence with it.

In 2010, the National Governors Association Center for Best Practices along with the Council of Chief State School

Mathematical Knowledge 19

Officers published the Common Core State Standards (CCSS) for mathematics in an attempt to create a coherent set of knowledge and skills that students should have by the time they graduate from high school. Like the authors of *Adding It Up*, the authors of the CCSS[24] argue that both skill and understanding are important. They also state that "the development of the standards began with research-based learning progressions detailing what is known today about how students' mathematical knowledge, skill, and understanding develop over time." (p. 4). At times, these progressions take a different trajectory than is typical of mathematics curriculum. As an example, in a traditional progression of learning about fractions students would first learn basic concepts such as fraction equivalence, followed by addition, subtraction, multiplication, and division. Following the CCSS, however, they move from understanding $\frac{3}{4}$ as three copies of $\frac{1}{4}$, to understanding $\frac{1}{4}+\frac{1}{4}+\frac{1}{4}=\frac{3}{4}$, to understanding $\frac{1}{4}\times 3=\frac{3}{4}$. All of these ideas are introduced prior to adding fractions with different denominators, a topic that is arguably more challenging that any of the ones just listed because of the need to rename fractions using a common denominator.

In addition to the grade level standards, CCSS include a set of standards for mathematical practice. These include: (1) make sense of problems and persevere in solving them; (2) reason abstractly and quantitatively; (3) construct viable arguments and critique reasoning of others; (4) model with mathematics; (5) use appropriate tools strategically; (6) attend to precision; (7) look for and make use of structure; and (8) look for and express regularity in repeated reasoning. The practices build on prior work that has emphasized processes in mathematics, including NCTM's five process standards and the five strands of mathematical proficiency described in *Adding It Up*.

As was the case with prior attempts to improve mathematics education, such as New Math and NCTM's reform efforts that led to the Math Wars, the CCSS initiative has been met with some criticism and resistance from a number of sources. For example, frustrated parents have circulated on social media sites what they perceived to be convoluted homework problems. Of course, not every homework problem that claims to be consistent with ideas represented in the CCSS is so. At the same time, there are standards that ask students to use ideas that, when written on paper, may appear to be more complicated than the basic skill requires. I (Kristie) recall a car ride once with my oldest child, in the summer prior to her entering kindergarten, when I asked her what 5 + 6 equaled. After a pause, she said 11. "How did you know that?" I asked. Her response was that she knew 5 + 5 was 10, and since 6 was one more that 5, you needed one more to get 11. Yes, it can be argued that this method is more complicated than just recalling 5 + 6 = 11 (which she didn't know) or than holding up six fingers to count from 5 to 11. But perhaps, to my daughter it was easier. As one expert I interviewed once told me, "easy" is not always about fewer steps. Essentially, it is about how much mental effort needs to be exerted to solve the problem. Since my daughter knew 5 + 5 = 10, that starting point was easy for her. When I asked her why she did it that way instead of counting on from 5 to 11, she said it was "faster." And of course it was natural for her – she had come up with the strategy on her own.

Her method isn't surprising; Brownell found students using similar methods even after two years of participating in a drill-focused program.[25] In the CCSS, students are expected to be able to both "count on" and "make ten." In this case, the "make ten" strategy for 5 + 6 is 5 + 5 + 1. As adults, a "make ten" strategy would not be faster than simply recalling the fact that 5 + 6 = 11, but a young child may not have memorized that fact yet. This is not to say that we don't care about or encourage memorization of basic facts. Indeed, this kind of memorization makes things more efficient. An information processing theorist might say it frees up working memory so that the child can attend to other features of a problem. The question is what do we do with the mathematical thinking that the child brings to school? We address this issue in Chapter 3.

Mathematics educators Diana Lambdin and Crystal Walcott[26] argued that a kind of pendulum seems to swing in mathematics education, but that in fact there are important variations and lessons to learn from each cycle of change. Tensions between skill and understanding, content and the learner, process and product are ever present. The resulting debates can be painful to participate in but ultimately can result in good outcomes for children – the "two sides" are forced to articulate positions, for example. We learn a lot when people on each side of a debate passionately articulate held beliefs about what mathematics is and how to learn it.

NOTES

1 Walmsley, A. L. E. (2007). *A history of mathematics education during the twentieth century*. Lanham, MD: University Press of America.
2 Resnick, L. B., & Ford, W. W. (1981). *The psychology of mathematics for instruction*. Hillsdale, NJ: Erlbaum.
3 Hiebert, J., & Lefevre, P. (1986). Conceptual and procedural knowledge in mathematics: An introductory analysis. In J. Hiebert (Ed.), *Conceptual and procedural knowledge: The case of mathematics* (pp. 1–27). Hillsdale, NJ: Lawrence Erlbaum Associates.

Mathematical Knowledge

4   Brownell, W. A. (1947). The place of meaning in the teaching of arithmetic. *Elementary School Journal*, 47, 256–265.

5   Dienes, Z. P. (1960). *Building up mathematics*. London: Hutchinson Educational.

6   Brownell, 1947.

7   Resnick & Ford, 1981.

8   Bruner, J. S. (1960). *The process of education*. Cambridge, MA: Harvard University Press.

9   Herrera, T. A., & Owens, D. T. (2001). The "new new math"? Two reform movements in mathematics education. *Theory into Practice*, 40(2), 84–92.

10 Skemp, R. R. (1976). Relational understanding and instrumental understanding. *Mathematics Teaching*, 77, 20–26.

11 Hiebert & Lefevre, 1986.

12 Star, J. R. (2005). Reconceptualizing procedural knowledge. *Journal for Research in Mathematics Education*, 36(5), 404–411.

13 Siegler, R. S. (2000). The rebirth of children's learning. *Child Development*, 71(1), 26–35.

14 Star, J. R., & Newton, K. J. (2009). The nature and development of experts' strategy flexibility for solving equations. *ZDM – The International Journal on Mathematics Education*, 41, 557–567. doi:10.1007/s11858-009-0185-5

15 Star & Newton, 2009.

16 Booth, J. L., & Davenport, J. L. (2013). The role of problem representation and feature knowledge in algebraic equation-solving. *Journal of Mathematical Behavior*, 32, 415–423.

17 Wu, H. (1999). Basic skills versus conceptual understanding – A bogus dichotomy. *American Educator*, 1–7.

18 Rittle-Johnson, B., Siegler, R. S., & Alibali, M. W. (2001). Developing conceptual understanding and procedural skill in mathematics: An iterative process. *Journal of Educational Psychology*, 93(2), 346–362.

19 Cuoco, A., Goldenberg, E. P., & Mark, J. (1996). Habits of mind: An organizing principle for mathematics curricula. *Journal of Mathematical Behavior*, 15, 375–402.

20 Lockhart, P. (2009). *A mathematician's lament: How school cheats us out of our most fascinating and imaginative art forms*. New York, NY: Bellevue Literary Press.

Mathematical Knowledge 23

21 National Council of Teachers of Mathematics. (2000). *Principles and standards for school mathematics*. Reston, VA: Author.

22 Herrera & Owens, 2001.

23 National Research Council. (2001). Adding it up: Helping children learn mathematics. In J. Kilpatrick, J. Swafford, & B. Findell (Eds.), *Mathematics learning study committee, center for education, division of behavioral and social sciences and education*. Washington, DC: National Academy Press.

24 National Governors Association Center for Best Practices & Council of Chief State School Officers. (2010). *Common core state standards for mathematics*. Washington, DC: Authors.

25 Resnick & Ford, 1981.

26 Lambdin, D. V., & Walcott, C. (2007). Changes through the years. In W. G. Martin, M. E Strutchens, & P. C Elliott (Eds.), *The learning of mathematics, sixty-ninth yearbook* (pp. 3–25). Reston, VA: National Council of Teachers of Mathematics.

Two
Mathematical Habits and Practices

> Used to say he felt algebra emotionally – told me once he could not read through the Binomial Theorem without tears coming into his eyes – the whole concept, he said, was so shatteringly beautiful . . . wish I could have got into his world, somehow or other.[1]
>
> James Hilton, *Random Harvest*

INTRODUCTION

In the opening quotation, the narrator is pressed up against the glass of mathematics: his friend Pal sees the shattering beauty of the Binomial Theorem, but that beauty isn't available to the narrator. And if we opened this chapter with a statement of the Binomial Theorem, chances are that most readers wouldn't start weeping with the shattering beauty of the statement. And if we reminded you of the statement of the theorem and then asked you to plug in numbers mindlessly to "practice" using it, you might weep, but probably not because you were moved by its elegance.

Growing up as a diplomat's child, I (Sarah) was often a new arrival in countries where I didn't speak the language. Invariably, I would hear from native speakers, "I'm sorry you have to learn [Portuguese]. It is much harder than other languages." Each speaker was correct, in a way – to learn to speak like a native speaker of any language is extremely difficult.

Mathematical Habits and Practices

And native speakers know from the inside how complex the language is – How many exceptions! How many idioms! Even to get good enough at a language to be able to take a city bus, for example, or go shopping, or even to make friends, takes practice and care. But for most people, it's doable. Long before you're fluent, you can communicate, and have real conversations.

Art can be treated similarly. Somerset Maugham captures some of the other side of that pressed-up-against-the-glass feeling in his book *The Moon and Sixpence*.[2] The art dealer Dirk Stroeve speaks passionately to his wife, who doesn't understand how he knows that some art is "great" art:

> Why should you think that beauty, which is the most precious thing in the world, lies like a stone on the beach for the careless passer-by to pick up idly? Beauty is something wonderful and strange that the artist fashions out of the chaos of the world in the torment of his soul. And when he has made it, it is not given to all to know it. To recognize it you must repeat the adventure of the artist. It is a melody that he sings to you, and to hear it again in your own heart you want knowledge and sensitiveness and imagination.

And yet. An art teacher at a small public elementary school in Minnesota, Angie Ekern, does just that. She gives kids the opportunity to repeat the adventure of an artist: she has the students in her art classes spend months working on an interpretation of *The Starry Night* painting. Even the kindergarteners learn about techniques Van Gogh used, about composition, and about the discipline of art. She doesn't pretend that the appreciation "lies like a stone on the beach" for the careless student to pick up – the students work and work and work

26 Mathematical Habits and Practices

at it. And at the end of that unit their work is not going to the Metropolitan Museum of Art, but they can recognize Van Gogh's work anywhere, and they can appreciate it deeply.

Figure 2.1 A Kindergartener's Interpretation of *Starry Night*.

Mathematics is not different, in the following sense: to see the beauty of the subject – to get into the mathematician's world – you must repeat, in some way, the experience of the mathematician. That takes "knowledge and sensitiveness and imagination." And mathematics experts of many varieties see the wide expanse of the mathematical landscape, with all its complexity.

School mathematics has traditionally been even more like a foreign language in the sense that the rules always seem to be changing as you learn it. In elementary school, you first learned that you can't take 8 from 4; and then later that you *can* take 8 from 4, you just get a negative number. The rules always seemed to be shifting. Similarly, school mathematics

Mathematical Habits and Practices   27

can be filled with things to memorize, like FOIL – an acronym everyone seems to remember, even if they don't remember what it does. So many acronyms! So many rules! How could anyone ever learn the language of mathematics? Is it possible that it's just "not given to all to know it"?

An ever-increasing body of research suggests that it is very much possible to learn mathematics in ways that "repeat the experience of being a mathematician." But learning mathematics is different from learning art in one significant way: not only is it beautiful and worthy of learning for its own sake, the stakes are different for mathematics than they are for art. Knowing and appreciating art is not going to make or break a college application, or even a successful high school or college career, the way knowing Algebra can. So the pressure is on – and not necessarily pressure for experiences that are authentic in that they "repeat the experience of being a mathematician."

What would an authentic experience even look like? I (Sarah) will start with a story of an office mate in graduate school, who came in to the office with steam coming out of his ears: his preschool daughter had been given a book about shapes, and one of the questions was something like this:

Figure 2.2 Which One of These Is a Rectangle?

"There are two rectangles on this page," he yelled. "A square is a rectangle. What *is* this????"

28 Mathematical Habits and Practices

Since that day, at least a dozen mathematicians – including the one I am married to – have come to me furious about shapes books for children. They're boring. They're imprecise. They give very small children the idea that math is *only* about memorizing names of things, and often have the kids memorize the wrong things. Christopher Danielson, former middle school teacher and author of the blog talkingmathwithyourkids.com, decided to create a different kind of book about shapes: one that would allow kids to do mathematical thinking; one that even the crankiest mathematician could love. The book is called *Which One Doesn't Belong?*[3] Each page features a set of four shapes. Take the shapes on the cover, for example:

Image used with permission.

Many adults might instantly count the sides and decide that the pentagon is the one that doesn't belong. But children

Mathematical Habits and Practices 29

argue differently, and spoiler alert, you can make an argument that any one of the four shapes does not belong. Here are some examples I've heard from small children:

- The L doesn't belong, because the other three are shapes and that one is a letter.
- The L doesn't belong, because it has an "inside corner." (The L is the only one that has an "open part".)
- The one on the bottom left corner doesn't belong, because it's sitting on a side that's shorter than the other sides. (It's the only one that's on one of its sides, because THIS one is supposed to be on the bottom.)
- The one on the bottom left corner doesn't belong because it is "going this way." (It is leaning.)

The activities in the book provide – for small children, and even for adults – the kind of experience that Angie Ekern, art teacher, provides with her Van Gogh–inspired unit. Kids get to experience the work that mathematicians do in an accessible way – grappling with unfamiliar ideas and eventually putting language to those ideas. It's a different experience for fifth graders than it is for three year olds, of course. Fifth graders are more articulate about the differences, and they have more experience of formal learning of shape to be able to identify characteristics of certain shapes; in other words, their language can help them. A mathematician might look at this figure and think that the L-shape doesn't belong because it's "not convex," meaning that you can draw a line segments with two endpoints inside the shape but so that the line is not entirely within the shape itself. No kid is going to come up with that language, but they can approximate it and struggle to build their own language to use. They have to look at the structure of the shapes; they have to think through possibilities; they have to find language for ideas they have probably not expressed before. They do the real work of mathematics.

Mathematicians do this. They are immersed in the work of creating new mathematics, and of talking about ideas that require both careful use of existing language, and sometimes even the creation of new language. Children can do real mathematics, in the same way that they can learn to communicate in real ways in (even imperfect) Portuguese, or learn to appreciate and create art in an authentic way. It's not about becoming professional mathematicians or high school mathematics teachers: it's about really learning what mathematics is, and perhaps more importantly, what mathematicians and users of mathematics *do* so that they can do that work themselves. What tools do they use when they create or use mathematics? To that end, what is it that we want our students to be able to do? What tools do we want them to use?

There are so many things we want children to grow up to be able to do – we want them to be able to do mathematics in all the forms they find it. Let's face it: we also want them to score well on standardized tests like the SAT and ACT, do well in school math, and jump over any mathematical fences they find on their career paths. We want them to be able to do simple things, like choose good phone plans, and more complicated things like compare mortgages or make good decisions about finances, including calculations of reasonable risk. We want them to be able to evaluate reasonableness of calculations: not to blind-faith believe every statistic they read, or to throw the baby out with the bathwater and simply believe that statistics

Mathematical Habits and Practices

are Rorschach tests, able to be manipulated to serve any outcome desired by Wizard of Oz–like statisticians behind green curtains.

All those things are good outcomes of a solid mathematics education, but they are the tip of the iceberg of what learning mathematics – in ways that are true to the discipline – have to offer. The real benefits of learning and understanding mathematics extend far beyond the school content itself.

So what's the iceberg? Cuoco, Goldenberg, and Mark[4] write:

> Much more important than specific mathematical results are the habits of mind used by the people who create the results. . . . The mathematics developed in this century will be the basis for the technological and scientific innovations developed in the next one. The thought processes, the ways of looking at things, and the habits of mind used by mathematicians, computer scientists, and scientists will be mirrored in systems that will influence almost every aspect of our daily lives. If we really want to empower our students for life after school, we need to prepare them to be able to use, understand, control, modify, and make decisions about a class of technology that does not yet exist. That means we have to help them develop genuinely mathematical ways of thinking.

They created the phrase "Mathematical Habits of Mind" to describe these ways of thinking. For example, one habit of mind is "students should be tinkerers," which is such a lovely way of thinking about one thing that mathematicians (scientists, coders, and probably to some degree lawyers and many others) do. An example of tinkering in the foundational Habits of Mind paper is this:

Rather than walking away from the "mistake"

$$\frac{a}{b} + \frac{c}{d} = \frac{a+c}{b+d}$$

they can ask:

- Are there any fractions for which this is true?
- Are there any sensible definitions of "+" that would make this statement true?

It's an approach that doesn't gloss over the fact that kids need to know that in general that statement isn't true for fraction addition – but a Habits of Mind approach allows kids to interact with the ideas in creative and constructive ways. And it gives kids an opportunity to repeat the adventure of the mathematician.

The Habits of Mind framework, among other thinking from teachers, mathematicians, and mathematics educators, heavily influenced the development of the CCSS's "Standards for Mathematical Practice" described in Chapter 1. These Standards, adopted in most states, and influential in even in non-adoption states, "describe ways in which developing student practitioners of the discipline of mathematics increasingly ought to engage with the subject matter as they grow in mathematical maturity and expertise throughout the elementary, middle, and high school years."[5] People aren't simply born with or without the ability to employ these habits. Some of them are built in naturally to humans' experimental nature; some are developed with practice. And most important, if students have opportunities to develop and use those practices, they have a real chance to get into the world that James Hilton refers to in the opening of this chapter – one in which the Binomial Theorem is so beautiful, it could make you weep.

In the rest of this chapter, we focus on three mathematical habits that can be developed in children and that are core to the practice of mathematics but have uses far, far beyond the world of the discipline. The habits are:

- Seeking and Using Structure
- Using Language Clearly and Precisely
- Experimenting

These habits are not distinct: they overlap. In order to "make use of structure," for example, you might need to carry out some mathematical experiments. In the exposition that follows, we will spotlight each of these three habits in action.

It's also worth noting that seeking and using structure, using language clearly and precisely, and experimenting are all habits we use in our worlds, almost whatever we do. Developing the mathematical versions of these habits in mathematics can give us a lot of power in our lives.

What follows in this chapter owes a huge debt to Glenn Stevens and Ryota Matsuura (and many others) for their work in mathematical habits of mind, but especially to my EDC colleagues Al Cuoco, Paul Goldenberg, and June Mark, who first articulated the framework. Any mistakes are mine.

SEEKING AND USING STRUCTURE

Mathematics is the science of structure.

Glenn Stevens

Why bother learning to "seek and use mathematical structure"? Mathematicians talk about structure as being at the

34 Mathematical Habits and Practices

heart of mathematical work. Understanding mathematics does not simply mean being able to compute things, or follow the directions for using formulas. It means being able to see and use structures in mathematics.

The Oxford English Dictionary's[6] definition of structure is useful here: "an arrangement and organization of interrelated elements in a material object or system, or the object or system so organized." Deborah Schifter uses the phrase "mathematical structure" to refer "to those behaviors, characteristics, or properties that remain constant across specific instances."[7] When we talk about structure here, we are thinking of purposeful or systematic arrangements.

William Thurston, one of the best mathematicians in the United States, wrote a paper on doing mathematics called, "On Proof and Progress in Mathematics."[8] In it, he describes his experience of reading colleagues' mathematics papers: he doesn't need to read the details because he knows large pieces of the mathematics. He likens his approach to using a toaster: you don't need to read a manual, you just plug it in and rely on your experience of using toasters in the past. We would call this use of structure in action.

There are many ways to use mathematical structure in the practice of school mathematics. Here's a way in which looking at things from a structural point of view can save you some headache. This problem comes from the Making Sense of Algebra[9] project at Education Development Center:

Rewrite the following expression without parentheses:

$$3(99^2 - 1) + 8(99^2 - 1) - 11(99^2 - 1)$$

You could see the parentheses and have an automatic, knee-jerk reaction of "distribute!" But looking at the expression

Mathematical Habits and Practices 35

with "structure glasses," you notice that the stuff in the parentheses is all the same. So you can chunk the expression this way:

$$3[\text{stuff}] + 8[\text{stuff}] - 11[\text{stuff}]$$

Whatever the [stuff] is — even if it's toasters — that sum is zero.

In this case, using the structure of the equation as presented saves work. It isn't just a party trick, or an ingenious gimmick: it's making a good choice to use structure — from a mathematical point of view, it's like choosing to stay under the stairs during a tornado warning.

How might you teach students to look for structure in school? Although there aren't definitive answers to that question, it seems reasonable to assume that if kids don't know that mathematical systems *have* structures, they're unlikely to look for them. So part of school teaching needs to include systematic searches that look for and make use of structure. As a bonus, those searches often give students opportunities to "repeat the experience" of mathematicians, in the words of Somerset Maugham.

I (Sarah) will give two examples, both produced by the Education Development Center. The first is from the wiki site of a National Science Foundation funded elementary curriculum, Think Math!.[10] In this lesson, students play with arithmetic, and that play reveals underlying algebraic structures and relationships. As it is presented in on the website, the teacher draws a number line on the board, like this:

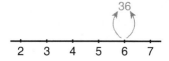

36 Mathematical Habits and Practices

The teacher then writes this:

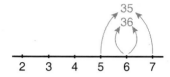

Adding (step by step) to the picture, the teacher ends up with something like this:

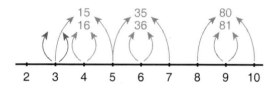

Images used with permission from Education Development Center, Inc.

In other words, an illustration of the following multiplication facts:

4 x 4 = 16

3 x 5 = 15

6 x 6 = 36

5 x 7 = 35

9 x 9 = 81

8 x 10 = 80

The students experiment with lots of examples, and eventually the teacher writes this up:

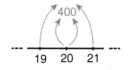

Mathematical Habits and Practices

What could 19 x 21 be? The students suspect that it must be 399.

Eventually they start to articulate something like this:

> (number x number) is always one more than (number – 1) (number + 1). Paul Goldenberg calls this "pidgin Algebra." Most students won't write the relationship down this way:
>
> $$x^2 = (x-1)(x+1)+1.$$

All these numerical calculations follow the same pattern, and that pattern can be captured with one general equation that captures all possible cases. This equation expresses an underlying structure in the number line – a surprising one.

Is there another way to see this underlying structure? There is. Draw an array picture of what 5 x 5 and 6 x 4 actually look like:

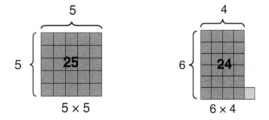

In the images, you see the relationships between the 5 by 5 square and the 6 by 4 rectangle: there's one extra square in the "square." You could draw similar arrays of 4 x 4 and 3 x 5, 6 x 6, and 5 x 7, 9 x 9, and 8 x 10, and you'd see pictures that look just like this one. Try playing with it. It's fun. Connecting across representations strengthens my (Sarah's) own understanding of underlying structures, and I've seen children

38 Mathematical Habits and Practices

light up at seeing those relationships, too. It's not that these representations are necessarily "structural," but looking at a collection of different representations gives kids a sense of the underlying structure that the representations are representing.

The next example is from the *Algebra* book of the high school mathematics curriculum CME Project.[11] Once again, the problem invites students to look for structure, building students' belief that there's structure to be found.

The curriculum asks students to explain any patterns they see in addition and multiplication tables similar to the addition table shown below. The tables are oriented a little differently from what students might be used to seeing in textbooks:

12	12	13	14	15	16	17	18	19	20	21	22	23	24
11	11	12	13	14	15	16	17	18	19	20	21	22	23
10	10	11	12	13	14	15	16	17	18	19	20	21	22
9	9	10	11	12	13	14	15	16	17	18	19	20	21
8	8	9	10	11	12	13	14	15	16	17	18	19	20
7	7	8	9	10	11	12	13	14	15	16	17	18	19
6	6	7	8	9	10	11	12	13	14	15	16	17	18
5	5	6	7	8	9	10	11	12	13	14	15	16	17
4	4	5	6	7	8	9	10	11	12	13	14	15	16
3	3	4	5	6	7	8	9	10	11	12	13	14	15
2	2	3	4	5	6	7	8	9	10	11	12	13	14
1	1	2	3	4	5	6	7	8	9	10	11	12	13
0	0	1	2	3	4	5	6	7	8	9	10	11	12
+	0	1	2	3	4	5	6	7	8	9	10	11	12

Many mathematical patterns emerge through their exploration. Students notice symmetry in the tables – because, for example, 3 + 4 and 4 + 3 are the same. I (Sarah) once worked with a student who said, "look, diagonals go up by two!" The language isn't precise yet, and no one is using phrases like "commutative property." But eventually, after students have found plenty of patterns and tried to articulate them, some of the patterns are named: a student might describe a pattern in this informal way: "one number plus another number is the same as the second number plus the first number." That's important! Through investigating and looking for patterns, they discover underlying properties – and those have names. For example, the student who said, "one number plus another number is the same as the second number plus the first number," was stating the rule known as "the commutative property." As a side note, the commutative property seems intuitive to adults: you don't think twice about rephrasing the question, "what's 5+3?" as, "what's 3+5?" But for early learners of mathematics, that's not trivial. 5+3 is the number that's 3 more than 5. 3+5 is the number that's 5 more than 3. It's not *totally* automatic that those are the same – when you use the sameness, you're using that commutative properties of addition of the real numbers – something structural about those numbers.

Likewise, my nine year old neighbor recently told me she was relieved that products like 9x7 and 7x9 were the same, because that meant she didn't have as much to memorize in her times tables. She's not explicitly thinking about that commutative structure of multiplication of real numbers, but she's using it well. Searching for and using structure is part of what mathematics is, and as that nine year old illustrates, it also makes school mathematics easier to learn.

USING LANGUAGE CLEARLY AND PRECISELY

Mathematicians use language carefully – it's part of why mathematics is often called "a language." In order to communicate about mathematics, you need to be able to speak precisely.

Mathematical Habits and Practices

In poetry, in literature, and in general conversation, communication captures experience, and human experience is not always logical or empirical. But mathematics aspires to the logical, to the empirical, so communication in mathematics is different.

Let's take the word "base," a word with many definitions. As an adjective, it means ignoble (when talking about a person or his actions) or not made of precious metals (when talking about jewelry). As a noun, the base of something is the foundation or the headquarters. It's also one of the stations that baseball players run around, and the white pillow-like thing at each station. And it turns out that bases are made of a material sometimes called "swag," another word with many definitions. Swag can also mean stolen goods or prizes. For a poet, this is a goldmine: imagine a line like, "base is not swag if stolen cunningly" – there are endless directions the poet can use with a line like that in a poem about baseball, say.

For a mathematician, this is a head-spinning language nightmare. Which base? Which swag? Mathematicians want words to mean what they say, and ideally mean *one* thing that can be stated precisely in a given mathematical context. Precision matters when you're trying to *prove* something, and mathematicians use definitions to prove things.

Here's an example of the usefulness of precise definitions: ask a few people whether zero is even. You may get a variety of answers. Some people will say that it's even, some people will say that it's neither even nor odd, and some people will say that being even or odd doesn't have anything to do with zero. Those answers are dependent on the individual's definition of an even number. If a person thinks "even numbers" are the set of numbers 2, 4, 6, 8, . . . then zero is not one of those. But is 5 million one of those? How do we know? A mathematician's

Mathematical Habits and Practices 41

definition of even number is an integer of the form $n=2x$, where x is an integer – in other words, even numbers are the ones that are divisible by 2. That's a definition we can work with: Is zero divisible by 2? Yes, because $0 = 2 \times 0$.

Beyond the fact that it's a core part of mathematical understanding, why bother to learn to use language clearly and precisely? We'll share examples with two aspects of clarity of language in mind: clear communication is useful, and also clear and precise definitions give students power to understand concepts (even acquire new ideas) and solve problems.

My (Sarah's) husband worked as a coder in the start-up boom of the late 1990s, and he communicates very much like a programmer. My children know very well that if they want him to get something from the grocery store, say, they have to communicate very clearly. If they want cookies and then specify the kind, he'll buy them. If they say, "can you get cookies?" he'll get the "most efficient" (i.e., cheapest) cookies he sees. One reason to bother with precision is simply better cookies – it's true not just for former coders, but for people in general. Clear communication matters.

But it's also a core part of programming, computer science, and all the hard sciences. Social science is enhanced by precise questions and communication. It's a core part of mathematics that – when taught well – can reach all aspects of a person's life. And like mathematical structure, learning to phrase questions mathematically, and learning to use mathematical language well, has strong implications for being able to *do* mathematics – not just talk about it.

There are so many important ways in which people rely on precision. Poetry aside, English teachers and professors frequently lament students' imprecise use of the word "it," because students are not always careful to use the word with any particular meaning in mind. Likewise, the pharmacist who prepares medication to give to patients needs to be precise both in the preparation and in subsequent communication to the patient: pharmacists are the front line of communication to patients about prescriptions.

With organizations like code.org and the programming language Scratch, children are growing up with more awareness of the importance of precision in the coding world, and with much more practice, too. But precision in mathematics is important, too.

The same is true for elementary and high school mathematics. When students learn to round, they are often give problems like, "round 16 to the nearest ten," or "round 230 to the nearest 100." Students sometimes memorize a rounding rule this way: "if you see a five, round up." If that's the rule students are using, it's not surprising that when asked to round 1,005 to the nearest thousand, students who use that rule answer "2,000." A more careful treatment of rounding teaches students to first take into consideration what they are rounding *to* – in this case, the nearest thousand. Paying attention to the *two* aspects of the problem – the number itself and what they are supposed to round to – makes the rounding relatively straightforward. That's the value of precision in the definition of rounding. (As a side note, elementary teachers will tell you that rounding procedures raise issues that students have with number sense, too.)[12]

For some students, Geometry courses are the first time they meet formal definitions, and the first time that they have the potential to see the *value* of precise definitions. For example, if students learn that "congruence means things are same," that's not very useful when they have to prove (say) that two triangles are congruent. If they learn instead what the

Common Core suggests: "For triangles, congruence means the equality of all corresponding pairs of sides and all corresponding pairs of angles," they have something to work with: they can check the lengths of corresponding pairs of sides and the angle measure of corresponding pairs of angles.

There's another aspect of precision and clarity that mathematicians care about very much; take a problem like this:

Solve $2x + 5 = 25$.

Some students might solve the problem this way:

$$25 - 5 = \frac{20}{2} = 10$$

While the student carried out a series of correct calculations to get to 10, the sentence "25 minus 5 equals 20 divided by 2 equals 10" is just not true. The student has the correct answer, but what he wrote down is *mathematically* incorrect because of the misuse of the equals sign. It isn't precise.

EXPERIMENTING

> You're not doing mathematics if you're not doing any experimentation.
>
> Ryota Matsuura

Most people typically think of experimentation as the domain of science. The truth is that experimenting is pervasive in our lives, and most of the time, for most of us, it happens outside of labs. Mathematics classes offer students opportunities to learn to do thought experiments and to build models. This happens in the world, too.

Sometimes experiments take place in our heads, and they lead to practical, immediately applicable solutions. The first time I (Sarah) saw Kristie pack a car trunk, she stared at her boxes for a while, and then stared at the trunk. She was running thought experiments in her brain, visualizing how the boxes might fit. Then she smiled and slid all the boxes neatly into the small trunk.

All children experiment. To babies and toddlers, the whole world is one giant lab. It's easy to see elementary schoolers, intent on building strong and complex sand castles, experimenting with ratios of sand to water to make good sand castle cement.

And numbers provide wonderful opportunities for experimentation. Take the following problem, for example, found in many places, including the NRICH mathematics website[13]: Some numbers can be written as the sum of two or more consecutive whole numbers.

This lends itself to play – just starting out trying some numbers. To start the second, you might make a systematic list:

$$
\begin{aligned}
1 &= 0+1 \\
2 &= \text{nope} \\
3 &= 1+2 \\
4 &= \text{nope} \\
5 &= 2+3 \\
6 &= 1+2+3 \\
7 &= 3+4 \\
8 &= \text{nope} \\
9 &= 4+5 \\
10 &= 1+2+3+4
\end{aligned}
$$

And so on. You might conjecture that powers of 2 cannot be written as the sum of two or more consecutive integers. But

Mathematical Habits and Practices 45

what on earth could a power of 2 have to do with sums of consecutive integers? You might even start to wonder about more things: are there other patterns you can find? Working on a problem like this invites an experimental approach, and allow students to experience mathematics the way a mathematician does, and experiment in ways that suggest mathematical structure.

This can and does happen for young children in mathematics, too. Cuisenaire Rods[14] allow kids to experiment with lengths and numbers.

46 Mathematical Habits and Practices

The images above show a four-year-old child playing with Cuisenaire Rods. First she lined them up, tallest to shortest. Then she started looking for how she could put them together in pairs: without doing any actual counting, she lined up the rod of length 9 with the rod of length 1, the rod of length 8 with the rod of length 2, and so on. She tried many, many times to put the rods together so that each rod had what she called a "friend," but she could never find a "friend" or the rod of length 5, so she moved that rod off the puzzle board. She then realized she could put the rod of length 5 together with the rods of length 2 and 3, but then she couldn't figure out what to do with the rods of length 8 and 7. She didn't like that, either. (As a side note, the fact that the rod of length 10 didn't have a friend didn't bother her at all.) Eventually, she just stuck the rod of length 5 across the side of rest of the rods, and she was happy. But in the meantime, she was setting the stage for looking at collections of numbers that add to 10.

Like using structure and careful language use, experimentation allows students entry to challenging mathematics. In our culture, "moving trains" word problems are considered the bane of many SAT-takers. The movie *How I Got into College*[15] has a few scenes in which characters from word problems (particularly moving train problems) harass the movie's hero. In the children's book *The Mysterious Benedict Society*,[16] one of the young characters "solves" a moving trains word problem by insisting that the engineers driving the trains would stop before they met. But experimenting can help. The eighth CCSS standard may sound somewhat mysterious: "look for and express regularity in repeated reasoning," but we'll illustrate what it is and how to use it to make those train problems and many others tractable. This is another method used in the high school curriculum CME Project.[17]

Let's consider one of those so very hated distance word problems. Here's an example the *CME Project Implementing and Teaching Guide*[18] uses as an illustrative example:

> Mary drives from Boston to Chicago and then drives back to Boston. She travels at an average rate of 60 mi/h on the way to Chicago and 50 mi/h on the way back. If the total trip takes 36 hours, how far is it from Boston to Chicago?

The CME approach is just to take some guesses. So a kid could guess something totally unreasonable, like 100 miles:

He's not trying to take a *correct* guess, he's trying to take a guess that will give him some insight about how to solve the problem.

48 Mathematical Habits and Practices

> guess: 100.
>
> $$50 \overline{)100}^{2}$$
>
> $$60 \overline{)100}^{1.\overline{6}}$$
> $$\phantom{60\overline{)}}\underline{-60}\downarrow$$
> $$\phantom{60\overline{)00}}400$$
> $$\phantom{60\overline{)0}}\underline{-360}$$
> $$\phantom{60\overline{)000}}40$$
> $$\phantom{60\overline{)000}}\vdots$$
>
> $2 + 1.\overline{6} = 3.\overline{6}$ hours
>
> no.

He wasn't sure after checking this guess what his equation was, so he took another guess:

> Guess 2: 1000 miles
>
> $$50 \overline{)1000}^{20}$$
>
> $$60 \overline{)1000}^{16.\overline{6}}$$
>
> $20 + 16.\overline{6} = 36.\overline{6}$ hours
>
> no

Mathematical Habits and Practices 49

He continued to guess until he could write down a "guess checker" (that is, an equation):

$$\left(50\overline{\smash{)}\text{guess}}\right) + \left(60\overline{\smash{)}\text{guess}}\right) = 36$$

$$x \div 50 + x \div 60 = 36$$

This student didn't read the problem and try to write down an equation. He read the problem and pretended that he had the answer. It's much easier to check an answer in a problem like this than to generate an equation. But as he checked answers, an equation started to emerge. In a more complicated problem, you might have to check more answers before an equation emerges, but the same principle applies. You repeat calculations until you're able to "express regularity" — in this case, express an equation that represents the question.

CONCLUSION

In this chapter, we took a close look at three ways of thinking about and doing mathematical work: structural approaches, language approaches, and experimentation. In the original paper that introduced Mathematical Habits of Mind,[19] Cuoco, Goldenberg, and Mark described a "bag of facts" approach to learning mathematics:

> One reason for this has been a view . . . in which mathematics courses are seen as mechanisms for communicating

established results and methods – for preparing students for life after school by giving them a bag of facts.

That bag of facts, no matter how full, is simply not a very satisfying possession. Mathematician William Thurston, in describing his real contribution to the field of mathematics, wrote:

> What mathematicians most wanted and needed from me was to learn my ways of thinking, and not in fact to learn my proof of the geometrization conjecture for Haken manifolds.[20]

In other words, even mathematicians do not seek bags of facts or static information. As students of the discipline, mathematicians reach for the insight that comes with learning ways of thinking. The learning of mathematics cannot be divorced from building the ways of thinking, habits of mind, and practices that are core to the discipline.

NOTES

1 Hilton, J. (2013). *So well remembered, random harvest, we are not alone: Collected novels*. New York, NY: Open Road Media.
2 Maugham. S. (1975). *The moon and sixpence*. London: Heinemann Educational Books, 68.
3 Danielson, C. (2016). *Which one doesn't belong?* Portland, ME: Stenhouse Publishers, 2017.
4 Cuoco, A., Goldenberg, E. P., & Mark, J. (1996). Habits of mind: An organizing principle for mathematics curricula. *Journal of Mathematical Behavior*, 15, 375–402.
5 National Governors Association Center for Best Practices & Council of Chief State School Officers. (2010). *Common Core State Standards for Mathematics*. Washington DC: Authors, 20.

6   *Oxford English Dictionary Online.* Retrieved from www.oed.com [Accessed August, 2016].

7   Schifter, D. (2018). Early algebra as analysis of structure: A focus on operations. In C. Kieran (Ed.), *Teaching and learning algebraic thinking with 5–12-year-olds: The global evolution of an emerging field of research and practice.* New York, NY: Springer.

8   Thurston, W. (1994). On proof and progress in mathematics. *Bulletin of the American Mathematical Society,* 30(2), 161–177.

9   Goldenberg, G., Mark, J., Kang, J. Fries, M., Carter, C., & Cordner, T. (2015). *Making sense of Algebra.* Portsmouth, NH: Heinemann Educational Books.

10   EDC, Inc. (n.d.) Difference of Squares. Retrieved from http://thinkmath.edc.org/resource/difference-squares. [Accessed July, 2016].

11   Education Development Center, Inc. (2009). *CME Project: Algebra 1.* Boston, MA: Pearson.

12   Martin, M., Meerts, G., Oehmke, C., Tyler, S., Matsuura, R., & Sword, S. (2017). Teachers voice: How collaboration helps us put research into practice. In L. West & M. Boston (Eds.), *Annual perspectives in mathematics education 2017: Reflective and collaborative processes to improve mathematics teaching* (pp. 51–60). Reston, VA: National Council of Teachers of Mathematics.

13   University of Cambridge. (1997–2018). Consecutive Sums Poster. Retrieved from https://nrich.maths.org/7999 [Accessed August 20, 2017].

14   The Cuisenaire Company.

15   Shamberg, M. (Producer), & Holland, S. S. (Director). (1989). *How I got into college.* [Motion Picture]. Los Angeles, CA: Twentieth Century Fox Film Corporation.

16   Stewart, T. L. (2008). *The mysterious benedict society.* New York, NY: Little, Brown Books for Young Readers, 9.

17   Education Development Center, Inc. (2009). *CME Project: Algebra 1.* Boston, MA: Pearson.

18   Education Development Center, Inc. (2009). *Guide to implementing and teaching CME project.* Boston, MA: Pearson, 37.

19   Cuoco, Goldenberg, & Mark, 1996.

20   Thurston, 1994, 176.

Three
Children's Thinking About Mathematics

If we are interested in helping children learn mathematics, it is important to understand their thinking about it. What do they know before they begin school? How do they reason about mathematical situations? What kinds of errors do they make? Children do not enter the classroom with blank mathematical slates, and teachers can be more effective if they build on children's prior knowledge and natural ways of thinking about mathematics. Although very young children do not typically have much experience with the syntax of mathematics, they do encounter and use mathematical ideas in their lives. But research suggests it is more than just exposure to mathematics (say, by a parent or caregiver); there is strong evidence that they are "primed" to learn it. And they like it.

EARLY AWARENESS OF NUMBERS

I (Kristie) recall one of my daughters, as a toddler, walking around the yard one day looking for particular kinds of sticks. At one point she had one in each hand, and she announced "Two!" with excitement in her voice as she continued walking and scanning the yard for more. Children do generally love to play with sticks, but in this particular moment there was something exciting about the quantity of her set of sticks. She had found *two* of them. Even more fun was when she noticed a picture of my mother and her identical twin and

Children's Thinking About Mathematics 53

announced there were "Two grandmas!" She was old enough to talk, but children notice quantity long before they have the words for it. Psychologists interested in the origins of number concepts study infants' noticing of small sets of objects. As early as 6 months of age, infants can discriminate between two and three objects in a set, as long as these sets are presented visually (e.g., black dots on a white page) and at the same time.[1] Evidence of this kind suggests that number sense may be innate.

More recently, psychologists have been interested in how and to what extent young children develop an awareness of how things are organized and related. Joanne Mulligan and colleagues refer to this as Awareness of Mathematical Pattern and Structure (AMPS).[2] Across the early years of schooling, this awareness manifests similarly across a wide range of tasks including number tasks, measurement tasks, and tasks that involve algebraic reasoning. AMPS can be measured in reliable ways, and it is positively related to learning outcomes for mathematics. Given the importance structure in the field of mathematics, this is an exciting area of emerging research.

Early awareness and understanding of mathematics can be seen in children's everyday play. Mathematicians "play" with numbers all of the time. When children do it, it may not look like the mathematics we think of in school, but children engage in pre-mathematical thinking quite frequently during their play. They sort toys by color. They use blocks to build symmetrical structures. They share things equally or look to see who has more. They complete puzzles. They count while their friends hide. They notice who swings higher. They compare heights to find out who is taller. In one study young children were observed playing, without direction, and almost 50 percent of their play involved mathematics or pre-mathematical thinking.[3] It is natural for children. They learn about mathematics through play, and they incorporate mathematics they learn into their play. And these early experiences are important. In a meta-analysis of large studies from six different countries, pre-mathematical ability was the strongest predictor of later achievement. Interestingly, it was a better predictor of later reading achievement than was early reading ability.[4]

This is not to suggest that early sense of number always reflects adult thinking. One difference is that our early sense of numerical magnitude is not linear. Instead, when asked to estimate where numbers go on a number line, smaller numbers are more spread out than larger numbers, which tend to be bunched up. In other words, our natural sense of number is more logarithmic than linear.[5] Below is a number line from a four year old, with 3, 8, 10, 13, 23, 37, and 41 estimated on a number line with 1 and 50 labeled as the endpoints. Although it is certainly arguable that she ran out of room for the larger numbers, she did not complain about it. And her planning did not accommodate the limited space.

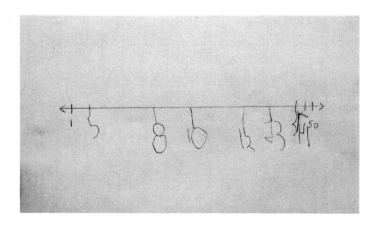

Evidence of mathematical thinking in young students is also not meant to suggest that preschoolers should be sitting at desks doing mathematics worksheets. Even in kindergarten, they can be off-putting for some students. One teacher I (Kristie) knew called them "games" to ease the distaste, although this led to a handful of students to decide they must be optional. And they opted out. Yet those same students may have a favorite card game that involves mathematics, or they may voluntarily play a numbers app for a solid hour. And they may show genuine interest when a new mathematical idea is being introduced. Exploring a new mathematical idea can be a playful thing to do. It's interesting to find patterns and make connections, *to experiment and make use of structure*. Practice plays a role in mastery of the new idea, something we return to in Chapter 4. But first, let's see what happens when children are asked to think about and solve new problems.

STUDENT-INVENTED PROCEDURES

Imagine yourself walking into a new classroom and not being able use your knowledge of classrooms in general to make sense of things. How confusing would this be? You might wonder why there needs to be so many "tables" in one room. You could question why they are so small or why they are all facing the same direction (or in any particular configuration). Fortunately, even in an unfamiliar classroom you can recognize desks, chairs, books, and other things that fit nicely into your current understanding. You recognize the objects that you expected to see, and everything feels okay. This recognition happens with mathematics as well. A student who is asked to find the sum of 1,549 and 361 can solve the problem based on prior knowledge of others like it, even if he or she has never encountered that particular one before. Upon seeing the multi-digit whole numbers, there is a sense of familiarity and a particular procedure comes to mind.

Psychologist Jean Piaget was highly influential in our thinking about sense making and about the cognitive development of young children. He is often associated with *constructivism*, a broad term used to describe a variety of related beliefs about how we learn. According to Piaget, we like to be in a state of balance, or equilibrium.[6] To maintain this balance, we respond to experiences through the processes of *assimilation* and *accommodation*. We assimilate information when we incorporate it into our existing frameworks, such as walking into a new space and recognizing it as a classroom. We may do something similar when we see a new type of mathematics problem. Students who first encounter decimal addition may decide that 2.3 + 5.6 = 7.9 based solely on their understanding of whole numbers, paying little attention to the decimal point. In this case, they happen to be correct. On the other hand, a similar process of applying whole number knowledge to $\frac{1}{2} + \frac{1}{4}$ would lead to an incorrect response of $\frac{2}{6}$, where students erroneously add numerators and then add denominators as if they were presented with two separate addition problems. In other words, the process of assimilation may or may not provide us with trustworthy information; it simply means we have used our existing frameworks to make sense of a situation. Accommodation occurs when we adjust our existing frameworks to account for new information. Even for the decimal example above, accommodation is necessary for learning since a student using his or her knowledge of whole number addition won't likely know how to find 5.02 + 3.1, perhaps guessing it would be 5.33 (lining up digits from the right) instead of 8.12 (lining up according to place value).

Children's Thinking About Mathematics   57

Asking students to make sense of new mathematical situations has led to some interesting insights about their thinking. When children are presented with school tasks such as word problems, they can often find solutions without formal instruction. In fact, they solve them in surprisingly predictable ways. Below is a word problem and a first grader's solution to it.[7]

> Braden has 6 stickers. Michael has 7 stickers more than him. How many stickers does Michael have?

Here is her solution:

58 Children's Thinking About Mathematics

On a different day the student was asked what 6 + 7 equals. She gave a slight pause and said 13. When asked to explain she said, "I know 7 + 7 = 14, and 6 is 1 less than 7 so it has to be 13." Yet, for the word problem she first drew the stickers, and then she counted them all and placed 13 in the rectangle to the far right. Finally, she filled in the remaining shapes with the "problem" (6 + 7). Representing the word problem with a numerical expression had been her final step in the following progression:

1. Read the problem and make sense of what it is asking.
2. Model the situation with a drawing.
3. Use the drawing to find a solution.
4. Translate the drawing into a numerical expression.

Contrast that process with this one:

> Mary has 14 stickers. She buys another 6 stickers. How many stickers does she have now?

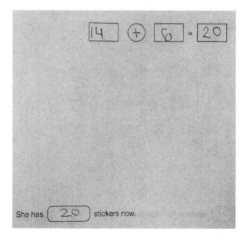

In this case, she translated the word problem into a numerical expression without the help of a drawing. Then she used the numerical expression to obtain the solution, which involved counting on from 14 to 20 with her fingers. Seemingly, this problem was the easier one. What is the difference between them? Are they not both simple addition problems? If anything, wouldn't the second one be more challenging, since it includes a two-digit number?

The work of Thomas Carpenter and colleagues[8] demonstrated that children do not think of addition and subtraction word problems in the same ways as many adults. They described four different classes of word problems that elicit different strategies from children. Two of these, Join problems and Separate problems, involve action. The other two, Part-Part-Whole problems and Compare problems, have no action; instead, they involve relationships between quantities. The first word problem above is an example of a Compare problem because it involves a comparison of two distinct sets of object — Michael's stickers and Braden's stickers. In this case, the compared quantity is unknown. Comparison problems can also have unknown referents or unknown differences. If instead we were told that Braden has 6 stickers and Michael has 13 stickers, the question might be "How many more stickers does Michael have?" This problem has an unknown difference, and a quick way to solve the problem would be to subtract (13–6). As an aside, children are sometimes told to think of addition when they see the "key" word *more*. Clearly, that trick just does not work! Sometimes *more* involves addition, and sometimes it does not. This example is one of many that illustrates why teaching word problems using "key" words is not recommended.

60 Children's Thinking About Mathematics

The second word problem above is a "Join" problem where the result of the joining is unknown. In particular, 14 stickers are being joined with an additional 6 stickers, and students was asked to find the total number of stickers. It is a problem type that the student had likely encountered many times. Her need to directly model the solution with objects had been replaced with a counting strategy. Likely, the student *could* model the solution with a drawing, but she also had another strategy available to her. As described with the Overlapping Waves Theory in Chapter 1, children often know more than one way to solve problems, and with experience they begin to use more efficient strategies.

Based on their research, Carpenter and colleagues urged teachers to build on the knowledge students bring to the classroom, so that instruction is better aligned with students' natural ways of doing mathematics. Their professional development program was known as *Cognitively Guided Instruction*. The program gained prominence during the same time that NCTM forwarded its ideas about problem solving and student thinking. But as the *Math Wars* revealed, there was disagreement about how far to take such an approach. Critics argued that efficient algorithms and fact memorization are important, that you don't want kids using cumbersome arithmetic algorithms forever – no matter how nifty. If single-digit multiplication is still using a lot of brain space, adding fractions is going to be a misery. Mathematician Paul Goldenberg says you really only need to memorize fifteen multiplication facts in order to free up working memory – this working memory allows kids to do the "good stuff" of higher order learning.

Of course, it is possible to believe that building on student thinking and learning efficient algorithms are both important. One challenge is reconciling what students naturally do when they are asked to make sense of contexts, with the rules we expect for them to know and carry out in school. Student-invented procedures do not always lead directly to the traditional way of solving problems in school. In one study where students invented ways to solve contextualized division problems, their efforts led to the *common denominator* method.[9] This method is a specific case of dividing across, with fractions expressed using common denominators so that dividing across denominators always results in a quotient of 1. So, in essence, if the denominators are the same, the process is to divide the numerators. If the denominators are not the same, you can use equivalent fractions to ensure denominators are the same. If the numerators do not divide evenly, the final quotient is a fraction. For example:

$$\frac{2}{7} \div \frac{3}{7} = 2 \div 3 = \frac{2}{3}.$$

On the other hand, in school children may learn to "flip and multiply", which looks like this:

$$\frac{2}{7} \div \frac{3}{7} = \frac{2}{7} \times \frac{7}{3} = \frac{14}{21} = \frac{2}{3}.$$

If children's natural ways of thinking about problems are not reconciled with the methods they are expected to use in school, they may be left believing that mathematics is not supposed to make sense. Thus goes the chant, "Ours is not to question why, just to flip and multiply."

ERRORS AND MISCONCEPTIONS

Once students begin to learn mathematical procedures in school, they are bound to make errors. Some of these errors are what we call "careless" because the student was rushed or just not careful, making an error he or she typically does not make. "Oops, I forgot the negative sign" is an example of this kind of error. We all make these errors, and students generally appreciate the partial credit that some teachers give in these cases. Other errors represent a conceptually based, persistent pattern. For example, a student may have a misconception such as thinking that subtraction is commutative. In this case, he or she may switch numbers around when it is convenient to do so. When faced with 40–34, a student with this misconception may treat 0–4 as equivalent to 4–0, giving 14 as a solution rather than 6. Edward Silver[10] referred to these kinds of predictable, conceptually based error patterns as *"systemic bugs."* When students invent their own algorithms, presumably they understand those algorithms and therefore the "bugs" are reduced, although not entirely eliminated.[11]

Those who argue for conceptual understanding of mathematics suggest it also leads to better retention of ideas and greater ability to transfer the learning to new situations. Poorly understood ideas can lead to poorly memorized algorithms and persistent errors. For example, when dividing fractions some students will "flip" the divisor but not change from division to multiplication. Or they might switch to multiplication but flip the dividend rather than the divisor. Other errors involve a "correct" algorithm that was misapplied. Students might, when multiplying fractions, "cross multiply" – a process sometimes used to check whether two fractions are equivalent.

Children's Thinking About Mathematics

I (Kristie) once heard a student refer to cross multiplication as the "butterfly method":

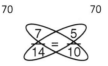

and then watched as a colleague easily convinced the student his method was not good, that he instead should be using the "dragonfly method":

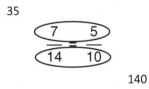

This new method was nonsense, but the student readily accepted it! Why? One might question this colleague's techniques, but the point he explicitly made to the student was that it is important to understand the mathematics. Don't just accept it as true, he said. Ask why it is true. If you don't understand why, he claimed, you are not as likely to remember how or when to use it. Without understanding, mathematical knowledge can be on shaky ground, fluctuating between butterflies and dragonflies.

When simplifying $4(x + 5)$, students may multiply 4 times x but forget or fail to multiply 4 times 5. This error leads to $4x + 5$ rather than $4x + 20$. Understanding why you need to distribute the 4 to both the x and the 5 can help. One teacher said she helps students understand by asking them to think of multiplication as repeated addition. Since 4 is being multiplied by $(x + 5)$, then $4(x+5)$ can be thought of as finding four copies of x+5. In other words, $4(x+5) = (x+5) + (x+5)$

+ (x+5) + (x+5). With some legitimate re-arranging we find that 4(x+5) = 4x + 4(5). In other words, there are four x's but also four 5's being added. Therefore, we distribute the 4 to both the x and the 5. While it is true that a student can understand this and still at times forget to distribute to the second term, such occasional forgetting would be a careless error and not a systemic bug.

As illustrated with the butterfly method, a *lack* of errors does not necessarily imply a student has a solid understanding of a mathematical procedure. A student may correctly cross multiply to determine if two fractions are equivalent but then use the same method to multiply fractions. And some students who correctly add fractions using common denominators also use a common denominator when it is not appropriate to do so, such as when multiplying or dividing fractions. For example, a student may correctly say $\frac{5}{7}$ is the sum of $\frac{2}{7}$ and $\frac{3}{7}$ but then erroneously find $\frac{6}{7}$ to be the product – multiplying the numerators but keeping the denominator the same. This error pattern has been found with both multiplication and division problems, across a range of ages and abilities[12,13]. It suggests a misconception that the choice of procedure is related to the likeness of denominators rather than to the mathematical operation.

Not only do students sometimes misapply algorithms to superficially similar problems (e.g., keeping the denominator when multiplying fractions with the same denominator) but they may also misapply algorithms based on the way the problem is presented. Near the beginning of one lesson I (Kristie) observed, a teacher posed $\frac{1}{2}+\frac{1}{4}$ by stacking the fractions vertically, one above the other:

$$\begin{array}{r}\frac{1}{2}\\+\frac{1}{4}\\\hline\end{array}$$

This vertical stacking effectively served as a visual trigger to remind students to rewrite $\frac{1}{2}$ as $\frac{2}{4}$ (typically written to the right of $\frac{1}{2}$). Next the students appropriately added the numerators to get $\frac{3}{4}$. Later in the same lesson, the teacher wrote the problem on the board in a horizontal fashion:

$$\frac{1}{2}+\frac{1}{4}$$

This time, the students added numerators and denominators to get $\frac{2}{6}$, despite having the correct answer still displayed on a different part of the board! This move was intentional by the teacher, as he was testing his suspicion that the students had linked the form of the problem with an algorithm rather than making a connection between the algorithm and the operation (addition, in this case). Typically, fraction multiplication problems are written in this same side-by-side fashion; it facilitates the process of multiplying numerators and multiplying denominators just as the stacking facilitates rewriting the fractions using a common denominator. Yet, the form in which the problem is written is not what determines the appropriate algorithm. We can add fractions that are written in a horizontal fashion just as we can multiply fractions stacked one above the other. Yet, students try to find meaning in the patterns they see, a point to which we return below.

Mathematical Variability Principle and Errors

Consider what a toddler might think if you point to blue cup and say, "It's blue!" It is possible the child will draw the conclusion that "blue" is a label for the cup itself. On the other hand, if you show him a blue cup, a blue bowl, a blue toy, and a blue shirt then the concept of "blue" will be more apparent. Zoltan Dienes makes a similar argument for mathematical ideas. Dienes was a Hungarian-born mathematician and educator, credited with some influential ideas about the way we think about early learning of mathematics. One of his principles of learning, the *Mathematical Variability Principle*,[14] forwards a rather simple but powerful idea for presenting new concepts. Namely, it states that in the collection of examples the learner experiences for a concept, irrelevant aspects of the concept should vary in order for the most relevant ideas to be more apparent.

We want to elaborate on Diene's Mathematical Variability Principle here because it provides a helpful perspective for understanding a variety of errors and how they might be related to instruction. The principle adheres to the idea that we are naturally inclined to notice patterns and draw conclusions, so teachers need to be intentional with patterns in order to help students draw valid conclusions. Imagine a fifth-grade classroom where any time students are presented with common denominators, they have to keep them the same. Students need to also be asked to multiply fractions with the same denominator since the likeness of denominators is not important for multiplying fractions and should therefore be an aspect that varies. Similarly, it is not critical that fraction addition problems be written in a vertical manner (it merely facilitates renaming the fractions with common denominators); therefore, fraction addition problems should sometimes be presented horizontally.

A similar idea applies to learning about shapes. For example, some very young children know that △ is a triangle but insist that ▽ is not a triangle or if it is, it is upside down. Consistent with the Mathematical Variability Principle, students should see triangles with different orientations and with a variety of angles and side lengths so that the common attribute – three sides – is more apparent to the student.

As another example, a child who is always provided with two side lengths to find area of a rectangle and four side lengths to find perimeter may not know what to do if asked to find perimeter based on only two out of four side lengths. The child may erroneously multiply these two dimensions, perhaps with a misconception that if you are given two numbers, you multiply. Alternatively, the child may add the two lengths rather than finding the missing lengths and adding all four, indicating a possible misconception that for perimeter, you add what is provided to you. In both cases, the focus is on what to do based on a particular trigger or superficial condition of the problem. Instead, we need students to think of perimeter as a measure of the distance around a closed figure. Yes, this often means adding up all of the side lengths, but there may or may not be four of sides for a given object. And calculating perimeter can involve multiplication, if some of the sides are the same length. In this case, multiplication provides a shortcut to adding several sides lengths that are the same, as with a rectangle:

P = 2l + 2w

w

l

Or with a regular hexagon:

P = 6s

s

In other words, the method for finding perimeter can change, but it always involves finding a total distance. That part doesn't *vary*.

The equals sign provides another example of where variation is needed. A widespread misconception of this symbol exists among young students that sometimes persists into middle school or even beyond.[15] Specifically, some students view the equal sign as an indication to provide an answer, as opposed to an indication that two numbers or expressions such as 2 + 4 and 6 have the same value. Ask a group of fifth graders to find the missing value for a problem such as 2 + 4 = ___ + 3, and many will respond with 6 by adding the 2 and 4. Another popular choice is 9, for which students add all the numbers without regard to their placement within the equation. One possible explanation for this misconception is that, for years, students are presented with problems in the form a + b = ____ and their job is to find the sum. From this pattern, they may conclude that the equal sign just signals you to provide an answer. Following Dienes' Mathematical Variability Principle, teachers should vary what is not important in order for students to notice what is important. In this case, the placement of the missing value is not important, so this should vary across problems. Students should sometimes see problems written in other forms, such as

____ = a + b

or

a + ____ = b.

What is common across the problem types is that both sides of the equation have the same value, thus the idea of equivalence is more apparent. Consistent with this principle, the CCSS recommend that students should have exposure to a variety of numerical equations in order to foster a more precise understanding of the equals sign.

The Role of Definitions

Many of the above examples stress the importance of definitions. As illustrated in Chapter 2, definitions are not trivial or inconsequential. When students in a middle or high school classroom are asked "What is area?", a typical response is "length times width." While it is true that this formula can be used to *calculate* area, it does not tell you what area *is*. Moreover, this formula is restricted to rectangles. Although the students would generally agree if you made these points and insisted on precise language, it is notable that the formula rather than the idea comes to mind first. If, instead, "area" brought to mind the total number of square units that cover a closed figure, the question of how to find this total would naturally follow.

Lack of a precise definition can cause confusion, or worse. Likely the topic most associated with negative emotions in elementary school is fractions. When asked what a fraction is, a common response is that it is "part of a whole." While this is certainly a critical idea, another definition is that a fraction is a real number in the form of a/b where a and b are real numbers and b ≠ 0. Simply put, a fraction is a particular kind of number. When students think of fractions as only part of a whole, any mention of a fraction may invoke images of pizzas, apples, and brownies. It is not our intent to suggest these images are entirely problematic. They are in fact useful representations of fractions that can help students ground their understanding in a familiar aspect of the real world. At the same time, a much broader conception is needed to more fully understand that fractions are numbers. In addition to the part of a whole interpretation, fractions can be interpreted as the answer to a division problem. For example $2 \div 3 = \frac{2}{3}$. A fraction can also be interpreted as a ratio, which is a comparison of two quantities. Even the part-whole interpretation is more complicated that the pizza imagery suggests. Fractions can be used to describe part of a region, part of a length, or part of a set of objects.[16] No wonder it is a confusing topic!

When fractions are defined as particular kinds of numbers, it can also help students understand their relation to whole numbers. Students learn whole numbers first and focus heavily on them for many years. When fractions are introduced, students understandably attempt to fit this new knowledge into their existing mental framework; they initially make errors with fractions based on their knowledge of whole numbers such as adding numerators and denominators for fraction addition. Instead they need to expand the framework.

Robert Siegler and colleagues describe an Integrated Theory of Numerical Development that elaborates on this process. This theory posits that the development of numerical knowledge involves a gradual expansion and refining of how numbers are defined. It "involves coming to understand that all real numbers have magnitudes that can be ordered and assigned specific locations on number lines"[17] (p. 274). Whereas defining fractions as part of a whole brings a cloud of mystery to fractions such as $\frac{9}{8}$, thinking of fractions as numbers on a number line can help students see that improper fractions are a natural extension of fractions less than 1. And it lays the foundation for understanding of number systems in general.

So far, we have shared various conceptions of what it means to understand and do mathematics, as well as ways that children think about mathematics. Given this groundwork, we turn our attention to what these ideas mean for learning to solve mathematics problems in school.

NOTES

1 Mix, K. S., Levine, S. C., & Huttenlocher, J. (1997). Numerical abstraction in infants: Another look. *Developmental Psychology*, 33(3), 423–428.
2 Mulligan, J. T., & Mitchelmore, M. C. (2013). Early awareness of mathematical pattern and structure. In L. English & J. Mulligan (Eds.), *Reconceptualizing early mathematics learning* (pp. 29–45). Dordrecht: Springer.
3 Ginsburg, H. P., Inoue, N., & Seo, K. H. (1999). Young children doing mathematics: Observations of everyday activities. In J. V. Copley (Ed.), *Mathematics in the early years* (pp. 88–100). Reston, VA: National Council of Teachers of Mathematics; Washington, DC: National Association for the Education of Young Children.
4 Duncan, G., Dowsett, C., Classens, A., Magnuson, K., Huston, A., Klebanov, P., Pagani, L., . . . Japel, C. (2007). School readiness and later achievement. *Developmental Psychology*, 43, 1428–1446.

Children's Thinking About Mathematics

5 Siegler, R. S., Thompson, C. A., & Opfer, J. E. (2009). The logarithmic-to-linear shift: One learning sequence, many tasks, many time scales. *Mind, Brain, and Education*, 3, 143–150.

6 Resnick & Ford, 1981.

7 Frank Schaffer Publications. (2009). *70 must-know word problems, grades 1–2 (Singapore Math)*. Columbus, OH: Author.

8 Carpenter, T., Fennema, E., Franke, M. L., Levi, L., & Empson, S. B. (1999). *Children's Mathematics: Cognitively Guided Instruction*. Portsmouth: Heinemann.

9 Sharp, J., & Adams, B. (2002). Children's constructions of Knowledge for fraction division after solving realistic problems. *The Journal of Educational Research*, 95(6), 33–380.

10 Silver, E. A. (1986). Using conceptual and procedural knowledge: A focus on relationships. In J. Hiebert (Ed.), *Conceptual and procedural knowledge: The case of mathematics* (pp. 118–198). Hillsdale, NJ: Lawrence Erlbaum Associates.

11 Carpenter, T. P., Franke, M. L., Jacobs, V. R., Fennema, E., & Empson, S. B. (1998). A longitudinal study of invention and understanding in children's multidigit addition and subtraction. *Journal for Research in Mathematics Education*, 29(1), 3–20.

12 Siegler, R. S., Thompson, C. A., & Schneider, M. (2011). An integrated theory of whole number and fractions development. *Cognitive Psychology*, 62, 273–296.

13 Newton, K. J., Willard, C., & Teufel, C. (2014). Struggling sixth grade students' ways of solving fraction computation problems. *Elementary School Journal*, 115(1), 1–21.

14 Dienes, 1960.

15 Alibali, M. W., Knuth, E. J., Hattikudur, S., McNeil, N. M., & Stephens, A. C. (2007). A longitudinal examination of middle school students' understanding of the equal sign and equivalent equations. *Mathematical Thinking and Learning*, 9(3), 221–247. doi:10.1080/10986060701360902

16 Kieren, T. (1988). Personal knowledge of rational numbers: Its intuitive and formal development. In J. Hiebert & M. Behr (Eds.), *Number concepts and operations in the middle grades* (pp. 53–92). Reston, VA: National Council of Teachers of Mathematics.

17 Siegler, Thompson, & Schneider, 2011.

Four

Learning to Solve Mathematics Problems

No matter your view of learning and doing mathematics, we can likely all agree it involves problems. We solve problems when we use mathematics in "real" life, we solve them for fun, and we solve them to learn. By the end of their school years, students have solved thousands and thousands of them. Indeed, it is difficult to imagine a mathematics classroom where students learn mathematics without solving any mathematics problems. But "problem" and "problem solving" are terms that mean different things to different people. For some, "problem solving" evokes memories of challenge problems, perhaps reserved for Fridays or for those who complete a test early. For others, it means the oft-dreaded real-world application problems that come at the end of the practice set. Still others hold entirely different meanings for these terms. Do these differences matter? What do they suggest for students learning to do mathematics?

WHAT IS A MATHEMATICAL PROBLEM?
Problems vs. Exercises

Psychologists, mathematicians, and mathematics educators are all interested in mathematics learning, but the questions they ask and the perspectives they take sometimes differ in important and even fundamental ways. For example, a psychologist studying mathematical learning may refer to any

74 Learning to Solve Mathematics Problems

problem-to-be-solved as a mathematical "problem," in contrast to a *worked example* that students study and discuss (described in more detail below). On the other hand, mathematics educators tend to make a distinction between *problems* and routine *exercises*. Exercises involve practicing a skill you have already learned, whereas a good problem is one you don't already know how to solve. From this perspective, the same task could be considered a problem for one person but not for another. Take for example, this one:

> After selling some brownies at a bake sale, you have $4\frac{1}{6}$ pans left for a party. If your guests only eat $1\frac{4}{6}$ pans of brownies, how many pans do you have left for yourself?

For most adults or anyone who has learned about subtracting mixed numbers, this task can be considered an exercise despite the fact that it is contextualized in terms of a bake sale. If, on the other hand, you know how to add mixed numbers but not subtract them, this task can be considered a problem – but one that is within reach. The last point is critical. According to Lev Vygotsky,[1] learning happens when tasks are within a child's *Zone of Proximal Development* (ZPD), which is the gap between what the child can do alone and what he or she can do with some assistance from an adult or more able peer. If instruction is aimed below the ZPD, learning does not take place because the child can already do the task. "Therefore, the only good kind of instruction is that which marches ahead of development and leads it; it must be aimed not so much at the ripe as the ripening functions." (p. 188). However, if the task is something the child cannot do even with assistance, it can lead to frustration.

The distinction between problems and exercises is important if you are interested in problem solving as described by NCTM during the Standards-based movement. From this perspective, problem solving is a way to get to understanding, not just something you do after you understand. It is through the problem solving process that understanding develops. For some curricula, the distinction means using rich, authentic tasks to uncover important mathematical ideas. Using the Connected Mathematics Project (CMP), you might be asked how much weight a bridge can hold given a particular thickness or length.[2] Or you might ask what type of packaging would be best for a product you are selling. As such problems are solved, the mathematical ideas are uncovered and then formalized and practiced. Videos from the Trends in International Mathematics and Science Study (TIMSS) highlight how a single problem can drive an entire lesson in some countries,[3] much like some of the standards-based curricula in the United States. This approach differs significantly from a more traditional one in the United States, where the teacher demonstrates an algorithm and then the students practice using it themselves, followed by a few contextualized problems to apply the ideas.

In the examples above, problem solving involves real-world contexts. One reason for contextualizing a problem is that students may have prior knowledge of the context that they bring to bear in making sense of and solving the problem. Another reason is to help students to see how the mathematics might be useful or important. According to the *Expectancy-Value Theory* of achievement motivation,[4] achievement and achievement-related behaviors such as effort and persistence are related to: (1) how well an individual *expects to do* at the given task, and (2) how much he or she *values* the task. Recall the algebra student who kept crumpling up his paper and throwing it on the floor. He did not expect to be able to understand or successfully complete the work he was given, so he was not motivated to put in any effort or time into it. Yet according to this theory, students might also fail to put in effort or persist with challenging work if they do not value it. Contextualized problems can provide value; they can help answer the enduring "When will we ever use this?" question. Although, as with the rocket problem, not all contexts will feel personally useful or meaningful to all students, some students might find a particular context to be important or interesting, thus finding value in it.

Real-world contexts are not necessary for students to find value in mathematical tasks. There are many who argue that mathematics is a worthwhile and interesting endeavor in its own right – even "shatteringly beautiful." Some students like the appeal of computing and knowing their computation will lead to a solution, while others love the patterns and become excited when they discover new ones. Some students may simply want to know the answer to a particular mathematical question or task and therefore engage in finding it. Asking students to make conjectures about mathematical ideas can spark this kind of intrinsic interest, and these kinds of tasks can also be problems in the above sense. If students in a class have learned to multiply fractions but not divide them, then asking them to divide two fractions might be an appropriate problem; it is something they do not already know how to do yet it is within reach. When I (Kristie) observed a teacher pose this question, all of the students in her class had the same conjecture: divide the numerators and divide the denominators.[5] Specifically, they claimed that:

$$\frac{8}{21} \div \frac{2}{3} = \frac{4}{7}$$

They further explained that 8 ÷ 2 = 4 and 21 ÷ 3 = 7. What is fascinating about this response, aside from the fact that they all agreed on it (which rarely happened in this classroom), is that I have heard adults argue that the method does not work or that they never thought of it that way. Yet, it was intuitive to these students. How did they know it worked? It was reasonable. They knew how to multiply fractions. They knew the relationship between multiplication and division. Most importantly, they had never been taught "Ours is not to question why, just to flip and multiply."

Asking the students to conjecture about dividing fractions prior to teaching them a method required that they activate prior knowledge and apply it to a new but related situation. In this case, their solution method was not the traditional one, but it was valid. Subsequent questions from the teacher helped the students understand that their method of dividing across was not always smooth; if the numbers did not divide evenly (and most do not!) then the method became cumbersome. As a result, the students were primed to learn an alternate method – one that works similarly in all cases. This teacher taught the students to use the traditional "invert and multiply" method, using contextual problems and tasks involving manipulatives in order to support conceptual understanding. She did not feel tied to a single instructional approach but instead adhered to NCTM's Representation standard,[6] which emphasizes the use of different representations and an ability to move between them. In the end, some of the students were also able to flexibly move between the two algorithms, choosing the one that best fit the situation. Recall this type of flexibility is considered to be an important aspect of procedural fluency.

Some might argue that it easier or more efficient to tell students to invert and multiply upfront rather than having them explore first. Perhaps it is. But without the opportunity to think about why we do not generally just divide across (but that we can!), a student's sense that mathematics is reasonable can be undermined. As one pre-service elementary teacher stated about dividing across, "No. It's impossible. If it was correct, why would anyone use the complicated invert-and-multiply algorithm?"[7] (p. 14). Pre-service secondary mathematics teachers have also questioned its validity, saying it must be a coincidence or it must only work in special cases. The disbelief from these older (college) students is striking, given that the younger students, who had not yet been taught a specific method, knew it made sense to divide across. Moreover, having an opportunity to explain and figure out how it works may lead to better retention and transfer of learning to new situations.[8]

In Project SEED, providing opportunities for this kind of figuring out is a mainstay of instruction. Instructors are trained to teach upper elementary school students using a Socratic style, asking only questions. Students are introduced to mathematical ideas they have yet to encounter in their regular classrooms, and instructors pose questions that guided their thinking. One pivotal problem posed in the fifth-grade curriculum is $2^0 = \_\_$. Most typically, the conjectures include 0 and 1. Students defending 1 point to the pattern in the powers of 2 chart, stating that, as the exponents decrease by 1, the answer is cut in half. Since $2^1 = 2$ and half of 2 is 1, then 2^0 must be 1. Students defending 0 point out that the exponent indicates how many times you multiply the base, so you multiply it zero times in this case. Coupled with this explanation, students often noted that $2 \times 0 = 0$.

If students are unable to resolve the issue after hearing these explanations, the instructor then would pose another

Learning to Solve Mathematics Problems 79

question for consideration; typically, one which contained 2^0 and could be solved using prior knowledge, such as $2^0 \times 2^5 = $ ___. Prior knowledge in this case was the rule that stated, when multiplying powers with the same base, you can add the exponents and keep the base the same. This rule was established prior to asking for the value of 2^0, so students generally agreed it was equivalent to 2^5 because $0 + 5 = 5$. Using this mathematical sentence, it could be seen that 2^0 functioned like a 1:

$$2^0 \times 2^5 = 2^5$$
$$\downarrow \downarrow \downarrow \downarrow \downarrow$$
$$1 \times 32 = 32$$

Often, this new situation was sufficient to convince the students, but other similar problems could be posed if necessary. Clearly, this process was not quick. I (Kristie) was guilty myself of sometimes rushing the process. When I pushed them to say $2^0 = 1$ before they were ready, it simply didn't stick with them. These students would, the very next day, say once again it was 0. Simply put, without the "ah ha" moment, it wasn't as likely to be retained.

These "ah ha" moments were in some ways the point of the program. We aimed for these moments, which were often accompanied by students raising a hand and shaking it vehemently back and forth in the air, coming slightly out of the chair, and trying not to yell out with excitement. We wanted to help students view mathematics as something attainable (i.e., something they expected to do well in) and worthwhile (i.e., something they valued). In other words, our goals were in line with the Expectancy-Value Theory described at the beginning of this section. Moreover, we wanted students to pursue more mathematical opportunities at the high school level as a result of increased confidence and interest in the subject. In terms of mathematical proficiency described earlier, the goal was to foster a *productive disposition*. We used mathematical problems to do this. Because asking students to make conjectures was followed by asking them to justify their thinking, the approach also promoted adaptive reasoning. Students created "proofs" like the one above during every class period. Students were encouraged to play with the mathematics, to *experiment*, as discussed in Chapter 2. In short, we hoped they would come to see mathematics as something that was interesting.

Games also provide opportunities for de-contextualized-yet-interesting problems. People often love games and puzzles, even those are not in any way connected to the "real world" or their personal lives, and even when they are not compensated or rewarded for playing or solving them. The school curriculum *Transition to Algebra* uses number puzzles to introduce and motivate work on arithmetic computation.[9] Similarly, in the *Connected Mathematics Project 2*[54], sixth-grade students begin the study of prime numbers with *The Factor Game*. The idea of the game is that two students play together. One student chooses a number between 1 and 30 on a number grid. The player who chose the number gets that number of points, and the other player gets the sum of the factors of that number, not including the number itself. So if a student chooses 4 first, he gets 4 points, and his opponent gets 1+2=3 points, because 1 and 2 are the factors of 4. Students quickly see that 29 is a great first move because the person who chooses 29 gets 29 points and her opponent only gets 1 point. A number like 6 is a neutral first move because the player gets 6 points and her opponent gets the sum of the factors: 1+2+3=6. And 12 is a bad first move because the player gets 12 points and the opponent gets 1+2+3+4+6=16 points. After playing a few times, students see that there's something special about numbers that are divisible only by themselves and 1. And after a day of playing the game without the burden of any formal language, the teacher assigns a name to these numbers: prime numbers.

Instead of playing a game like this, students are often introduced to prime numbers with a definition:

> A prime number is a whole number greater than 1 whose only two whole number factors are 1 and itself.

Following the definition, you might ask students to decide which of a collection of numbers is prime, or maybe you start with some examples and then ask students to try some on their own. Likewise, many textbooks simply lay out rules of arithmetic in a kind of alphabet soup of variables and asks students to memorize them. In either case, students could reasonably ask something like, "When am I *ever* going to use this?"

What makes the Factor Game interesting is that students get a set of experiences that allow underlying structures to appear. Prime numbers are useful because they are good first moves in a game. Rules of arithmetic are meaningful because they emerge from kids' experiences. In both cases, the authors designed the experiences so that underlying structure would emerge. And seeing that structure emerge is thrilling. We talked about the importance of structure in Chapter 2, and games are a wonderful way to reveal mathematical structures.

Nice Problems

Mathematicians talk about "nice problems." According to one mathematician we talked to,

> deciding on criteria for what makes a "nice" problem is sort of like deciding on criteria for what makes a "good" men's professional basketball player. Of course you can think of certain things – probably at least 6'4", fast, nimble – but getting into the details gets so sticky that General Managers get paid millions of dollars to make those decisions. Nice problems are hard, but not *too* hard; their solutions contribute to the field; they are interesting to work on.

Fermat's Last Theorem offers an example of this: the statement is easy to understand, and for a long time, people have been pretty sure it was true. But knowing it was true wasn't going to change much in the field of Number Theory – and for a long time, it seemed like an intractable problem. In working on the solution, Andrew Wiles showed that the problem wasn't intractable, but even more important, the work that Wiles did on the proof of the theorem contributed significantly to the field.

Courant and Robbins[10] argue:

> Without doubt, all mathematical development has its psychological roots in more or less practical requirements. But once started under the pressure of necessary applications, it inevitably gains momentum in itself and transcends the confines of immediate utility. This trend from applied to theoretical science appears in ancient history as well as in many contributions to modern mathematics by engineers and physicists.

Learning to Solve Mathematics Problems

But just as mathematical "problems" don't require real-world contexts, real or practical contexts don't necessarily make a problem "relevant" or interesting to solve. I (Sarah) was once sitting in a friend's new kitchen, and she was talking about what it was like to buy her house. For her, the worst part of the experience was being presented with all of the information of the mortgage. "I'm a poet," she said. "Who could possibly expect me to make sense of all of that?" She just wanted someone else – someone trustworthy – to read the numbers, make sense of them, and tell her what to do. And as I was listening to her talk about what she saw (or didn't see) in all of those numbers, I was thinking about real-world mathematics. You can't get much more real-world than your mortgage payment. Those numbers were as relevant to her life as any she might encounter. But that mathematics didn't *feel* personally relevant to her. She just wasn't interested in them, even though she knew she *should* be, somehow.

I happened, that day, to have heard about a problem that I thought might capture the imagination of a poet. One of my colleagues at EDC, Bowen Kerins, presented a problem for pre-calculus students to investigate. The problem appears in the precalculus textbook of *CME Project*:

In a poem, the "rhyme scheme" describes the arrangement of rhymes at the end of each line, and is usually described by lower case letters, in alphabetical order. For example, consider a stanza of the Andrew Marvell poem "The Definition of Love"[11]:

> As lines, so love's oblique, may well
> Themselves in every angle greet:
> But ours, so truly parallel,
> Though infinite, can never meet.

The rhyme scheme is *abab*. A four-line poem with no rhyming lines would have rhyme scheme *abcd*. Bowen asked, "How many rhyme schemes could a four-line poem have?" And then he extended: "How many rhyme schemes could a five-line poem have? A poem with n lines?" So I asked my friend the poet these questions. She got interested in the mathematics, and started puzzling it out. At first she thought of herself as solving a problem about poems – she was thinking of actual poems she knew with different rhyme schemes. But soon she had abstracted to the combinatorial problem, and was just working on that. She got pretty far, actually, before she started thinking about dinner.

Problems vs. Worked Examples

For psychologists, a mathematical problem is generally something the student works out, as opposed to a worked example provided to the student to study. So, then, problem solving is what students do to find the answers to mathematics problems, be they routine exercises or more open-ended tasks. The distinction is important because the use of worked examples in laboratory and classroom settings have a rich history in the field of psychology. A worked example shows a problem and a solution method for students to examine. Researchers find that worked examples are most effective when they include questions to help students elaborate on or explain particular aspects of the example. Without the prompts to explain, learners with expertise on a particular problem type benefit more from solving problems on their own because the use of worked examples can impose unnecessary information to process. This situation is referred to as the *expertise reversal effect*.[12] A textbook example may or may not include any of these prompts for students.

Worked examples can be used in pairs, where students are asked to compare two side-by-side worked examples in order to highlight a particular idea. For example, students might be asked to compare a correct and an incorrect method in order to a target misconception. Or they might be asked to compare a general method that always works to a method that is more efficient but only works under certain circumstances, targeting flexibility. Or, to target conceptual understanding, they might be asked to compare two methods where one method demonstrates why the other one works. For example, one method for simplifying $2^3 \times 2^4$ is to add the exponents and keep the base the same. Another is to rewrite each term in expanded form to get $2 \times 2 \times 2 \times 2 \times 2 \times 2 \times 2$ and then rewrite the result as a power of 2. The latter method can be compared to the former method to understand why it works to add the exponents. A teacher using side-by-side worked examples should facilitate a discussion to highlight important ideas. In a year-long study of 141 Algebra I teachers, greater use of these kinds of side-by-side worked examples was related to greater procedural knowledge.[13]

Worked examples involving a single method are more common. To be most effective, they are paired with a prompt for students to self-explain. For example, rather than comparing a method to one that highlights why the method works, students might be asked instead to study a correct method and then prompted to explain why a particular step is valid. These worked examples can also be incorrect, and students might be prompted to explain why a particular step is not a valid mathematical move. Below, the worked example illustrates a common error with fraction addition. Students are asked to identify the error and think about how the incorrect response compares in size to the correct response. Research shows that this type of prompting increases conceptual knowledge.[14]

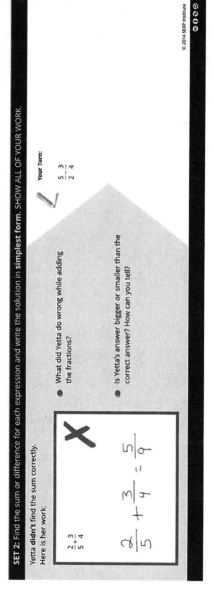

Figure 4.1 © SERP 2017 under CC BY-NC-SA 4.0. Included with permission. *serpinstitute.org*

Learning to Solve Mathematics Problems 87

The use of incorrect worked examples has been used to help correct persistent errors, and research shows they are especially helpful for students with lower prior knowledge. It is easy to assume that showing a struggling student an incorrect example will serve to confuse the student, but in fact there is evidence that these students are the ones who benefit most. Since these students are the ones likely making the errors they are studying, they can benefit from thinking about why the methods are not valid. In fact, when students first view an incorrect method, they may believe it is valid if it is the method they have been using. However, students with high prior knowledge also benefit from studying and explaining incorrect examples, in addition to explaining correct examples and to solving their own (routine) problems.

HOW DO WE SUPPORT STUDENTS IN LEARNING TO SOLVE PROBLEMS?

The Role of Cognitive Load

As the reversal effect implies, if you know how to effectively solve a problem, studying someone else's solution method may require more effort than just solving the problem yourself. On the other hand, the use of worked examples is meant to *reduce* the *cognitive load*, or mental effort, for students as they learn new ideas.[15] It is meant to make things easier. According to cognitive load theory, tasks have some level of cognitive load that is inherent in the task and therefore unchangeable. On the other hand, some things about the task are artificially demanding and can therefore be manipulated with instructional design (such as the use of worked examples). By studying a worked example, the mental focus can stay on understanding and discussing the mathematical idea or procedure rather than on figuring out what steps might work to solve it (particularly if the procedure is new and so the students has little or no information about how to proceed).

Of course, worked examples are not the only way to reduce cognitive load. Imagine trying to mentally calculate $1,567 \times 8$. Paper and pencil can make it easier without changing the nature of the problem itself. These tools can reduce cognitive load. Technology also offers huge opportunities for reducing cognitive load. The free graphing calculator Desmos (desmos.com) allows students to investigate, among other things, relationships between graphs of functions. Students can graph many functions quickly and look for relationships. This is not to suggest students shouldn't graph things by hand. But the dynamic nature of a graphing calculator drastically reduces the overhead in studying functions and their graphs. (See Fig. 4.2)

Touchscreens can also reduce extraneous cognitive load, for example, by making it easier to manipulate information. They are becoming more available as part of the mathematics classroom in middle schools and high schools, and many children have access to touchscreens at even much younger ages at home. Ryota Matsuura and Olaf Hall-Holt have been experimenting with representing and interacting with algebraic concepts, including polynomials, in this new context. In experimenting with children's learning about polynomials, they began with an emphasis on physical manipulatives that would lead into a more flexible virtual environment, and then moved to a tablet. Hall-Holt and Matsuura observed that a tablet interface provided comfort and familiarity to young students even when the app focuses on topics that the students have not seen before.

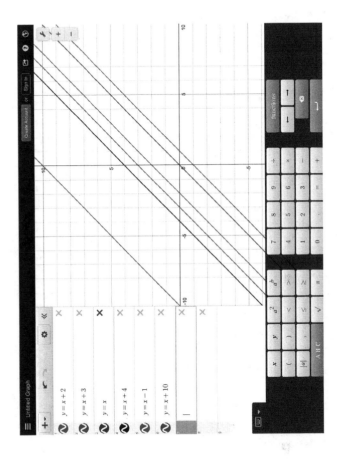

Figure 4.2 A Few Linear Functions Graphed in Desmos.

With all of these tools for reducing cognitive load, it may seem strange that mathematics educators sometimes talk about problem solving in terms of increasing the complexity of thought, or *cognitive demand*, required by the student. For more cognitively demanding tasks, students are asked to figure something out, based on some degree of prior knowledge. This process mimics what someone might do who uses mathematics in their career (e.g., the rocket scientist). To guide our thinking about posing tasks for students, Smith and Stein[16] described four levels of cognitive demand for mathematical tasks: memorization, procedures without connections, procedures with connections, and doing math. Memorization typically involves reproducing facts or formulas and is considered low on cognitive demand. For example, you might ask a student to tell you the formula for finding the surface area of a rectangular prism. Procedures without connections typically involves the use of an algorithm without any links to the underlying concepts. Asking a student to find the surface area of a rectangular prism given its length, width, and height might be considered this level of cognitive demand. These kinds of tasks are often used for practicing a new skill. On the other hand, procedures with connections requires some thinking about the underlying ideas. This kind of task might make use of representations, such as helping students see how a surface area formula is connected to a real object. Although these tasks are considered to require high cognitive demand, the highest level is doing math. When a student is "doing math," he or she had not been provided with a solution path. For example, asking a student to determine how much paper is needed to cover a box is "doing math" if the student has not yet been introduced to surface area. The student would need to notice that there are six rectangles that need paper, make the connection to area, and use his or her prior knowledge to find the area of each one. Likely, the student would then add all the areas together to find a total. This sort of task could be followed by an introduction to surface area and the formula for finding surface area of a rectangular prism.

Does the idea that we sometimes want to pose cognitively demanding tasks contradict the idea that we want to reduce cognitive load? The rocket scientist faces problems that are high in cognitive demand, but it doesn't mean he or she doesn't value and search for ways to make the job easier. Cognitive efficiency is generally valued among mathematics experts.[17] When asked to say why they prefer a particular method, a common response among experts is because it is "easier." Easier can mean fewer steps, but it can involve more steps if those steps help make the problem less mentally taxing (lower cognitive load). Recall the expert who automatically multiplied both sides of an equation by 3 in order to clear the denominator (Chapter 1). Although this method is arguably more efficient than distributing a fraction as a first step, he was genuinely upset when he realized there was an even more efficient way to solve problem. In his mind, the less cognitive load required, the better. This kind of efficiency is also preferred by novices. Recall the idea of figuring out that $5 + 6 = 11$ by starting with a known fact (i.e., $5 + 5 = 10$) and making adjustments for the new problem. This method was "faster" than "counting on" with fingers. Students who struggle with algebra also show a preference for solution methods that take less mental effort, even if they do not use them because they have a single method they rely on and feel comfortable with.[18]

So why, on the one hand, do we want to lower cognitive load while (at times) increasing cognitive demand? In addition to wanting to provide students with opportunities to experiment and be problem solvers, some degree of challenge can be motivating. On the other hand, too much unnecessary challenge can lead to frustration or disinterest. The notion of moderate challenge has been forwarded as a way to strike a balance with mathematical tasks in the classroom.[19] In order for challenge to be motivating, the task should be within reach (within the child's ZPD), and the classroom environment needs to be supportive. When teachers emphasize learning and effort and support students in reaching challenging goals, students are more likely to show interest and work hard to meet the challenges.

Scaffolding

When challenge is inherently high for a task, *scaffolding* can help. In a recent gymnastics practice of my (Sarah's) six year old, none of the girls could stay in a handstand because their backs were too arched. The coach had them do "handstands on the floor" (lying on the ground) so that gravity was doing the hard work, and then they could get the arches out of their backs. He kept moving them to more and more steeply sloped ramps on which they did "handstands" with less and less support, each time having them get the arches out of their backs on the ramps. Eventually they were all doing real handstands without arches in their backs – the whole thing took about 15 minutes. The coach's goal wasn't to "dumb down" the handstands – it was to put aside gravity as needed until they got the right idea – and then put them back up in handstands. It was fun to watch: the children were jumping up and down with excitement because they could feel themselves getting

Learning to Solve Mathematics Problems 93

stronger and stronger. This process of providing support and slowly decreasing it is often referred to as scaffolding.

Effective scaffolding in mathematics takes the child's prior knowledge into account so that the support is appropriate for that child.[20] In Chapter 1, Kristie described her daughter's process for adding 6+5, when she didn't know the "fact." She used her knowledge that 5+5=10, and then reasoned from there. Her daughter built that process for herself, but it's the kind of thing you can scaffold with children, too, and it's very useful for addition. What we've done in my (Sarah's) family is adapted from *Think Math* work on "pairs to ten." From a very young age, we asked our children to count how many fingers we were holding up. They would count. We also asked them to count how many fingers were "hiding." Eventually, they could see quickly how many fingers were visible and how many were hiding. We still play this game often, but we also sometimes just say, "6," and wait for the "4" that pops up. It's just a game. With our elementary-school-age daughter, we also play pairs to 20, pairs to 100, and even "pairs to a million." Starting with counting fingers is a really simple entree into pairs to 10. As a side note, that's also the work that the child in Chapter 2 is doing with Cuisenaire Rods: she's making pairs to 10. Representations can be helpful scaffolds, a point we return to shortly.

Mathematicians do this scaffolding for themselves. They conduct thought experiments. They look at concrete examples. They put in extra conditions. Mathematician Andrew Wiles proved Fermat's Last Theorem, and one thing that makes Wiles' proof interesting is that multiple people worked on it over decades. Many mathematicians laid down "stepping stones" – not as pedagogical tools, the way teachers use scaffolding, but as research tools towards a proof that seemed intractable. And that the final proof – because of the scaffolding – fits on the back of a t-shirt that students in a summer program called PROMYS made as a fundraiser. Hundreds of years of mathematics, on the back of a T-shirt!

Representations

Imagine the numbers 4, 40, and 400. In your mind, you might automatically link these numbers with some sort of image that reveals their relative size. But in looking just at the digits on the page, it is not obvious just how different these numbers actually are from each other. To a child just learning these symbols, it may not be apparent at all; in fact, their similarities may stand out as what is important. Yet comparing 4 and 400 is not unlike comparing 2 and 399, at least in terms of magnitude. Understanding whole number magnitude is important because it is linked to later performance in mathematics,[21] and one of the primary ways to make number magnitude apparent is by creating visual representations of the numbers.

Recall that *representation* is one of the NCTM process standards, which states that students should be able to create and use representations of mathematical ideas, translate between representations, and use them to model "real" situations. Concrete materials, diagrams, tables, and number lines are all examples of helpful representations. Recent standards have highlighted the importance of number lines in particular. Within the CCSS,[22] number lines are used in third grade as a way to emphasize that fractions are numbers. Number lines can also help students make sense of improper fractions. Placing $\frac{9}{8}$ on a number line isn't that different than placing $\frac{7}{8}$. on the number line, whereas they are quite different when using a circle representation because students need to know what to

Learning to Solve Mathematics Problems 95

do once their circle "fills up". Some students try to squeeze in the ninth $\frac{1}{8}$ rather than drawing a new circle. Using a number line representation can also help students focus on fraction magnitudes. Similar to knowledge of whole number magnitude, knowledge of fraction magnitude is important as it predicts later learning in mathematics, including algebra.[23] Knowledge of number magnitude in general seems to be a key component of mathematical learning, and it can be supported by using a variety of representations.

Base 10 blocks have long been popular for helping children learn and understand place value. These blocks, invented by Dienes, consist of units, longs, flats, and blocks that can be physically manipulated to help children count, add, subtract, multiply, or divide. When using these to represent numbers such as 4 (four units), 40 (four longs), and 400 (four flats), the role of place value is more salient. In Chapter 3 we described Dienes' Mathematical Variability Principle, which suggests non-essential aspects of a problem or idea should be varied to make the important aspects more apparent. Similar to this principle, his Perceptual Variability Principle encourages us to vary the different types of materials used for learning mathematical ideas. Consider, for example, a child that only ever represents fractions using circles. He or she may begin to think fractions can only represent areas, not lengths or set of objects. Or the child may conclude there is something about the circle in particular that is important. By exploring fractions with a variety of representations, the common features can be abstracted and understood as significant by the child.

In order to support children learning mathematics with meaning, Bruner believed that the way ideas were represented should change over time. He described three modes of representation through which students should move as they learn

96 Learning to Solve Mathematics Problems

new topics.[24] The first, enactive representation, involves actively manipulating objects as described above. To learn equivalent fractions a student may use fraction circles to find two different ways to represent half a circle. An advantage of using the physical objects is that they can be easily manipulated. For example, a child can pick up two-fourths and stack them on top of a one-half piece to confirm they are the same size. The second, iconic representation, involves icons or images such as using drawings of circles or rectangles to find two equivalent fractions. Although the diagram is visually similar to the concrete manipulatives, they are less dynamic. Finally, a symbolic representation of equivalent fractions would involve numbers, such as $\frac{3}{6} = \frac{2}{4}$. According to Bruner, these modes of representation mimic the stages infants and young children initially move through as they learn to interact with the world.

Although different representations help students to visualize and better understand mathematical ideas, ultimately we do need students to be able to think with and manipulate symbols. Otherwise, higher-level mathematics like algebra or calculus would be unattainable. It is not always easy for children to make this transition, however. In fact, it can be quite challenging, even when a student can successfully solve problems using concrete materials or diagrams. To illustrate, let's take a second look at the brownie problem from the beginning of this chapter. This problem can be solved using concrete representations such as pattern blocks. It goes something like this:

You begin with $4\frac{1}{6}$ pans of brownies.

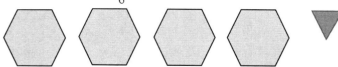

Learning to Solve Mathematics Problems 97

Next you try to remove $1\frac{4}{6}$ pans of brownies but find you need more sixths, so you split a whole brownie pan into six sixths.

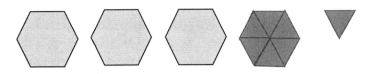

Finally, you are ready to remove $1\frac{4}{6}$ pans of brownies. Your solution is $2\frac{3}{6}$ or $2\frac{1}{2}$.

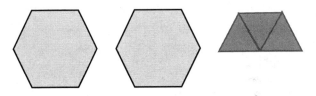

Unfortunately, students can succeed at this task but then stare blankly at the same problem written symbolically; the transition is not automatic. For the problem above, the symbolic representation might look something like this:

$$\begin{array}{r} 3\frac{7}{6} \\ \cancel{4\frac{1}{6}} \\ -1\frac{4}{6} \\ \hline 2\frac{3}{6} \end{array}$$

Students may need help to understand that replacing one hexagon with six triangles corresponds to crossing out the 4, writing a 3, and adding $\frac{6}{6}$ to the $\frac{1}{6}$ that was there to begin with. In short, although alternative representations support (and many would argue are necessary for) learning about symbols, they are certainly not sufficient.

Practice

We all hear that "practice makes perfect" but is it true for leaning mathematics? And what kind? How much? How often? Some of us have memories of doing twenty-five (or more!) practice problems for homework several times per week, while others may be accustomed to doing fewer problems less often. It is doubtful the rocket scientist spends much, if any, time practicing skills, but practice is generally viewed as a typical part of learning mathematics. The ideal amount of practice may vary across individuals, but there is evidence to support two ways to structure or organize practice.[25] The first, *distributed practice*, is practice that is spaced over time. Essentially, this principle is consistent with the idea that "cramming" for a test or quiz is not conducive to long-term retention of the material. The second, *interleaving*, is essentially mixed practice. When a student practices only adding fractions within a problem set, he or she may seem to know and understand the process. Mixing fraction addition with multiplication problems, however, requires that the student make a distinction between the problem types and associated solution methods. This additional attention toward thinking about the difference between the two problem types enhances learning.

CONCLUDING THOUGHTS

Our purpose in writing this book was to introduce some ideas about mathematics learning by drawing on three general perspectives: those of mathematicians, educational psychologists, and mathematics educators. Mathematicians of course are deeply versed in the content and in the practice of mathematics; educational psychologists are interested in mechanisms and processes involved in learning; mathematics educators are interested in tools and methods to facilitate learning mathematics in particular. At times in our history these voices have seemed to contradict one another when it comes to implications for the classroom. Project-based learning! Learning through "real" contexts! Drill, drill, drill! Memorize! Don't memorize! It would not be ground-breaking to suggest there is probably some truth in each of these ideas. Nor would it be new to suggest that perhaps mathematics learning is not a one-size-fits-all endeavor. Fortunately, efforts to reach across fields are increasing. Recently, a large group of mathematics educators, psychologists, and neuroscientists met to outline a research agenda for understanding mathematical cognition, with the purpose of providing more coherence to the work.[26]

These perspectives are by no means the only ones involved in decisions about mathematics learning and about the classrooms in which that learning takes place. Policy makers, textbook publishers, parents, and teachers are also among the many invested in mathematics education. Many teachers have vast stores of knowledge about mathematics learning that they are not in position to share because of time constraints. Federal funding trends have shaped the availability and selection of resources – a wave of funding for new curriculum projects, for example, led to the development of many of the curricula cited throughout this book. And recent partnerships led to the CCSS, which represents a huge effort by policy makers to bring best practices to schools, and to invite civic engagement around what mathematics is and how to learn it.

The ideas shared in this chapter are by no means the only ones related to mathematics learning. Carol Dweck writes about the importance of mindset – that simple things like telling kids that they are "smart" can reduce their willingness to take intellectual risks and thus hamper learning.[27] Jo Boaler and others write about the benefits of making errors.[28] Countless authors have written about the role of discourse in mathematics learning. Others write about the role of feedback as students learn to solve problems. Still others write about the roles of sociocultural factors such as gender, race, and socioeconomic status. The extent of interest and contribution to our understanding of mathematics learning is impressive; a comprehensive reporting is beyond the scope of this book, but we encourage interested readers to seek out this work. In this book, we set the stage for these more nuanced aspects of learning mathematics by addressing some of the fundamental ones. What is mathematical knowledge? What does it mean to learn and do mathematics? How do children think about mathematics? And how do we help them learn mathematics?

Although we focus primarily on learning mathematics, teaching and learning are clearly linked. In a recent handbook chapter, psychologist Julie Booth and her colleagues summarized research from cognitive science as eight principles that support mathematics learning, most of which we elaborate on in this book. These eight principles include representations, scaffolding, worked examples, comparison, error reflection, interleaved practice, distributed practice, and feedback. Some of these principles are geared toward sensemaking and understanding, such as comparison and error reflection. Others, such as distributed practice and feedback, are geared toward improving memory and fluency. Although understanding is often pitted against fluency, many would argue, as we do, that both are important. And we would be remiss if we were to say there is a best way to achieve these things for all students. The most effective teachers that we know artfully draw upon and integrate ideas from many sources and perspectives, and they alter these as appropriate for the many different learners in their classrooms.

NOTES

1 Vygotsky, L. S. (1962). *Thought and language*. Cambridge, MA: MIT Press.
2 Lappan, G., Fey, J., Fitzgerald, W., Friel, S., & Philips, E. (2006). *Connected mathematics Project 2*. Boston, MA: Pearson.
3 Stigler, J. W., & Hiebert, J. (1999). *The teaching gap: Best ideas from the world's teachers for improving education in the classroom*. New York, NY: Free Press.
4 Wigfield, A. L., & Eccels, J. S. (2000). Expectancy-value theory of achievement motivation. *Contemporary Educational Psychology*, 25, 68–81.
5 Newton, K. J., & Sands, J. (2012). Why don't we just divide across? *Mathematics Teaching in the Middle School*, 17(6), 340–345.
6 National Council of Teachers of Mathematics, 2000.
7 Tirosh, D. (2000). Enhancing prospective teachers' knowledge of children's conception: The case of division of fraction. *Journal for Research in Mathematics Education*, 31(1), 5–25.
8 Bruner, 1960.
9 Mark, J., Goldenberg, P., Kang, J., Fries, M., & Cordner, T. (2014). *Transition to algebra*. Portsmouth, NH: Heinemann.
10 Courant, R., & Robbins, H. (1996). *What is mathematics?* Oxford, UK: Oxford University Press.
11 Marvell, A. *The definition of love*. (poem) Retrieved from www.poetry-foundation.org/poems/44679/the-definition-of-love [Accessed August 21, 2017].
12 Kalyuga, S., Ayres, P., Chandler, P., & Sweller, J. (2003). The expertise reversal effect. *Educational Psychologist*, 38, 23–31.
13 Star, J., Pollack, C., Durkin, K., Rittle-Johnson, B., Lynch, K., Newton, K., & Gogolen, C. (2015). Learning from comparison in algebra. *Contemporary Educational Psychology*, 40, 41–54.

14 Barbieri, C., & Booth, J. L. (2016). Support for struggling students in algebra: Contributions of incorrect worked examples. *Learning and Individual Differences*, 48, 36–44.

15 Sweller, J. (1994). Cognitive load theory, learning, difficulty, and instructional design. *Learning and Instruction*, 4, 295–312.

16 Smith, M. S., & Stein, M. K. (1998). Selecting and creating mathematical tasks: From research to practice. *Mathematics Teaching in Middle School*, 3(5), 344–346.

17 Star & Newton, 2009.

18 Newton, K., Star, J. R., & Lynch, K. (2010). Understanding the development of flexibility in struggling algebra students. *Mathematical Thinking and Learning*, 12(4), 282–305.

19 Turner, J. C., & Meyer, D. K. (2004). A classroom perspective on the principle of moderate challenge. *Journal of Educational Research*, 97, 311–318.

20 Booth, J. L., McGinn, K. M., Barbieri, C., Begolli, K., Chang, B., Miller-Cotto, D., Young, L. K., & Davenport, J. L. (2017). Evidence for cognitive science principles that impact learning in mathematics. In D. C. Geary, D. Berch, R. Oschendorf, & K. M. Koepke (Eds.), *Mathematical cognition and learning Volume 3: Acquisition of complex arithmetic skills and higher-order mathematics concepts* (pp. 297–325). Oxford, UK: Elsevier.

21 Booth, J. L., & Siegler, R. S. (2008). Numerical magnitude representations influence arithmetic learning. *Child Development*, 79, 1016–1031.

22 National Governors Association Center for Best Practices, 2010.

23 Booth, J. L., Newton, K. J., & Twiss-Garrity, L. (2014). The impact of fraction magnitude knowledge on algebra performance and learning. *Journal of Experimental Child Psychology*, 118, 110–118.

24 Resnick & Ford, 1981.

25 Booth, J. L., McGinn, K. M., Barbieri, C., Begolli, K., Chang, B., Miller-Cotto, D., Young, L. K., & Davenport, J. L. (2017). Evidence for cognitive science principles that impact learning in mathematics. In D. C. Geary, D. Berch, R. Oschendorf, & K. M. Koepke (Eds.), *Mathematical cognition and learning. Volume 3: Acquisition of complex arithmetic skills and higher-order mathematics concepts* (pp. 297–325). Oxford, UK: Elsevier.

26 Alcock, A., Ansari, D., Batchelor, B., Bisson, M-J., De Smedt, B., Gilmore, C., . . . Webwe, K. (2016). Challenges in mathematical cognition:

A collaboratively-derived research agenda. *Journal of Numerical Cognition*, 2(1), 20–41. doi:10.5964/jnc.v2i1.10

27 Dweck, C. S. (2006). *Mindset: The new psychology of success*. New York, NY: Random House.

28 Boaler, J. (2015). *Mathematical mindsets: Unleashing students' potential through creative math, inspiring messages and innovative teaching*. San Francisco, CA: Jossey-Bass.

Glossary

Accommodation — altering one's existing frameworks in order to fit new information into them

Adaptive reasoning — the logical thought needed to justify mathematical moves

Assimilation — incorporating new information into existing frameworks

Cognitive demand — the complexity of thought required by a task

Cognitive load — the mental effort required by an individual to complete a task

Common denominator method — a way of dividing fractions that involves finding a common denominator and then dividing the numerators (e.g., $\frac{2}{7} \div \frac{3}{7} = \frac{2}{3}$)

Conceptual knowledge — a connected web of mathematical knowledge

Conceptual understanding — understanding how different mathematical ideas are related, how they are represented, and when they are useful

Constructivism — a broad term used to describe a related set of beliefs about learning that suggest humans actively make sense of their experiences

Count all — adding two sets by beginning with 1

Glossary

Count on — adding two sets by beginning with the total in the first set

Distributed practice — practice that is spaced over time

Expertise reversal effect — the finding that an instructional technique that is effective for a student with little or no knowledge of a topic can hinder performance for a student with high knowledge, perhaps due to an increase in cognitive load

Expectancy-Value Theory — theory of achievement motivation that posits that achievement and achievement-related behaviors such as effort and persistence are related to how well an individual expects to do at the given task, and how much he or she values the task

Flip and multiply — a traditional method for dividing two fractions which involves multiplying the first fraction by the reciprocal of the second fraction

Fraction — a real number in the form $\frac{a}{b}$, where $b \neq 0$

Instrumental understanding — knowing how to carry out procedures

Interleaved practice — practice that involves multiple skills; mixed practice

Math Wars — philosophical differences and debates about the relative importance of conceptual understanding and procedural knowledge

Mathematical proficiency — a perspective on mathematical understanding that involves five related strands: conceptual understanding, procedural fluency, strategic competence,

	adaptive reasoning, and a productive disposition about mathematics
Mathematical Variability Principle	one of Diene's four principles, which states that in the collection of examples the learner experiences for a concept, irrelevant aspects of the concept should vary in order for the most relevant ideas will be more apparent
Overlapping Waves Theory	a theory that can explain the movement from less mature methods that children might use (e.g., counting with fingers) to more sophisticated ones (e.g., recall)
Procedural flexibility	knowledge of multiple ways to solve problems along with the ability and tendency to choose the best method based on specific characteristics of the problem
Procedural fluency	knowledge of procedures and skill with using them both accurately and flexibly
Procedural knowledge	an important aspect of mathematical knowledge that includes knowledge of symbols, syntax, and algorithms
Productive disposition	seeing mathematics as something worthwhile, understandable, and achievable
Relational understanding	knowing not only how to calculate an answer but also why it works that way
Scaffolding	the process of providing instructional support and then slowly decreasing it as the learner gains knowledge of a topic
Strategic competence	Being able to represent a problem mathematically

Systemic bugs	predictable, conceptually based error patterns
Worked example	a mathematical problem and its solution presented to students to study and discuss
Zone of Proximal Development (ZPD)	the gap between what the child can do alone and what he or she can do with some assistance from an adult or more able peer

Index

Page numbers in italic format indicate figures.

accommodation 56, 104
achievement motivation theory 75, 105
adaptive reasoning 18, 80, 96, 104, 106
Adding it Up 17
additive inverses 6, 7
algorithms: about 3–4, 16, 17; efficient 60, 61; misapplied 62, 64; relational understanding of 10
assimilation 56, 104
Awareness of Mathematical Pattern and Structure (AMPS) 53

Back to Basics movement 8
base 10 blocks 95
Binomial Theorem 24, 33
Boaler, Jo 100
Booth, Julie 100
Brownell, William 4, 5, 20
butterfly method 63, 64

careless errors 62, 64
Carpenter, Thomas 59, 60
children: and early awareness of numbers 52–55; and mathematical thinking 28; and shape books 28; and word problems 47, 57–60; *see also* students
"clear the denominator" strategy 10
CME project 38, 47, 83
cognitive demand 90, 91, 92, 104
cognitive efficiency 91
cognitive load 87, 88, 91, 92, 104
Cognitively Guided Instruction program 60
Common Core State Standards (CCSS) 19–20, 32, 47, 94, 99
common denominators 8, 11, 61, 64–66, 104
communication in mathematics 40–43
"commutative property" 39
Compare problems 59
conceptual knowledge 9, 10, 13, 18, 104
conceptual understanding 17, 18, 62, 85, 104
congruence 42, 43
conjectures 6, 7, 14, 76–78, 80
Connected Mathematics Project (CMP) 2, 75, 80
constructivism 56, 104
contextualized problems 75, 76, 78
Council of Chief State School Officers 18, 19

Index

count all method 11, 104
count on method 11, 21, 105
cross multiplication 10, 62, 63, 64
Cuisenaire Rods 45, 46, 93
Cuoco, Al 14, 31, 33, 49
curriculum 7, 8, 16–17, 35, 93

Danielson, Christopher 28
definitions, role of 69–71
denominators: common 8, 11, 61, 66, 104; likeness of 64, 66; and numerators 56, 65, 70, 76
Dienes, Zoltan 4, 66, 69, 95
distributed practice 98, 100, 105
doing math task 43; as a level of cognitive demand 49, 90
Dweck, Carol 100

Education Development Center 34, 35
efficient algorithms 60, 61
Ekern, Angie 25, 29
enactive representation 96
equals sign symbol 68–69
equations 10, 12, 13, 35, 37–38
errors: careless 62, 64; and Mathematical Variability Principle 66–69; and misconceptions 62–65
even numbers 40, 41
exercises: vs. problems 73–81; routine 74, 84
Expectancy-Value Theory 75, 79, 105
experimenting as a practice 15–16
expertise reversal effect 84, 105

Factor Game 80, 81
federal funding 8, 99
feedback, role of 100

Fermat's Last Theorem 82, 93
flip and multiply method 3, 61, 77, 105
fractions: about 4, 8, 105; adding 9, 11, 19, 60, 66, 98; clear the denominator strategy for 10; definition issue 70; dividing 62, 64, 77; multiplying 64, 65; and problem solving 11; worked example 85, 86

games 80, 81
Geometry courses 42–43
Goldenberg, Paul 14, 31, 33, 37, 49, 60
graphing calculator 88, 89

habits and practices: about 24–33; CCSS standards for 19–20; conclusion about 49–50; experimenting 15–16, 43–49; for mathematical problems 98; for mathematics learning 3; role of 55; structures as 12–13, 33–39; types of 33; using clear language 39–43
Habits of Mind 32, 49
Hall-Holt, Olaf 88
Hilton, James 24, 32–33

iconic representation 96
information processing theory 3, 21
instrumental understanding 9, 105
integers 6, 7, 41, 44, 45
Integrated Theory of Numerical Development 71
interleaving practice 98, 105
"invert and multiply" method 77, 78

Join problems 59, 60

Index

K-12 curriculum *see* curriculum
Kerins, Bowen 83, 84

Lambdin, Diana 21
language, using clear 30, 39–43
learning *see* mathematics learning/teaching
Lockhart, Paul 14, 15
long-term memory 3

Making Sense of Algebra project 34
Marvell, Andrew 83
mathematical knowledge: about 1; and CCSS standards 19; and conceptual knowledge 9, 10, 13, 18, 104; and procedural knowledge 3–4, 106
mathematical patterns 38, 39
mathematical problems: about 73; conclusion about 98–101; description of 73; vs. exercises 73–81; and games 80; and nice problems 82–84; practice for 98; representations 94–98; scaffolding 92–94; vs. worked examples 84–87; *see also* problem solving
mathematical proficiency 18, 20, 80, 105, 106
mathematical symbols *see* symbols
mathematical thinking 5, 28, 53, 54, 55
Mathematical Variability Principle 66–69, 95, 106
mathematics: CCSS for 19–20; communication in 40–43; conceptual understanding of 62; early awareness of 53; and errors and misconceptions 62–65; as a "language" 39–40; precision in 40–43; and role of definitions 69–71; and student-invented procedures 55–61
mathematics learning/teaching: and being a mathematician 27; conclusion about 98–101; debate for 13–14; and focus on meaning 4–14; and focus on process 14–21; and focus on skill 1–4; instructional strategies for 8; and procedural flexibility 10, 12, 13, 106; and systematic searches 35; using clear language for 30; value of 2; *see also* habits and practices
Math Wars 17, 20, 60, 105
Matsuura, Ryota 33, 43, 88
Maugham, Somerset 25, 35
meaning, focus on 4–14
memorization 21, 60, 90, 99
misconceptions and errors 62–65
Moon and Sixpence, The (Maugham) 25
moving trains word problem 47
Mulligan, Joanne 53
multiplication facts 36, 60

National Council of Teachers of Mathematics (NCTM) 2, 16
National Governors Association Center for Best Practices 18
National Science Foundation 16, 35
negative numbers 6, 26
New Math movement 8
nice problems 82–84
number lines 6, 35, 54, 71, 94
numbers: early awareness of 52–55; even 40, 41; experimentation with 44–45; natural sense of 54; negative 6,

26; positive 6, 8; prime 80, 81; whole 56, 70, 81, 94, 95
numerators 9, 56, 65, 70, 76

"On Proof and Progress in Mathematics" paper 34
Overlapping Waves Theory 11–12, 60, 106

Perceptual Variability Principle 95
perimeter, calculating 67
Piaget, Jean 56
place value 56, 95
polynomials 88
positive numbers 6, 8
practice *see* habits and practices
pre-mathematical thinking 53, 54
prime numbers 80, 81
Principles and Standards for Mathematics 16
problem solving: about 16; and cognitive demand 90; and fractions 11; and real-world contexts 75, 76; support for 87–92; and worked examples 84–87
procedural flexibility 10, 12, 13, 106
procedural fluency 18, 105, 106
procedural knowledge 3–4, 9–10, 85, 106
procedures with connections 90
procedures without connections 90
process, focus on 14–21
Process of Education, The (Bruner) 5
productive disposition 18, 80, 106
Project SEED 6, 78
PROMYS program 94

real-world contexts 75, 76
rectangles 14–15, 27, 68–69, 90–91

relational understanding 9, 10, 15, 106
representations 94–98
rote memorization 4, 8, 15
rounding, treatment of 42
routine exercises 74, 84

scaffolding 92–94, 106
Schifter, Deborah 34
shape books 28
side-by-side worked examples 85
Siegler, Robert 11, 71
Silver, Edward 62
Skemp, Richard 8–9, 15
skill, focus on 1–4
standardized tests 4, 30
Starry Night painting 25, 26
Stevens, Glenn 33
strategic competency 18, 105, 106
Stroeve, Dirk 25
structure: defined 34; as a practice 12–13; seeking and using 33–39
student-invented procedures 55–61
students: assessment of 4; and CCSS standards 19, 20; and errors and misconceptions 62–65; and integers 6; mathematical thinking in 55; support for 87–92; as tinkerers 31; and worked examples 84–87; *see also* problem solving
student thinking 16, 60, 61
symbols 3–4, 13, 68, 96–98
systemic bugs 62, 64, 107

technology 31, 88
Think Math! curriculum 35, 93
thought experiments 43, 44

Index

Thurston, William 34, 50
tinkerers and tinkering 31–32
touchscreens 88
Transition to Algebra curriculum 80
Trends in International Mathematics and Science Study (TIMSS) 75
triangles 14–15, 42–43, 67, 98

vertical stacking 64, 65

Walcott, Crystal 21
Which One Doesn't Belong? (Danielson) 28
whole numbers 56, 70, 81, 94, 95
Wiles, Andrew 82, 93
word problems 47, 57–60
worked examples 84–88, 107
working memory 3, 21, 60

Zone of Proximal Development (ZPD) 74, 107